# BLACK BRITISH

# BLACK BRITISH

---

## *IMMIGRANTS TO ENGLAND*

R. B. DAVISON

*Published for*
*the Institute of Race Relations, London*
*by*
OXFORD UNIVERSITY PRESS
LONDON    NEW YORK    TORONTO
1966

*Oxford University Press, Ely House, London W.1*

GLASGOW NEW YORK TORONTO MELBOURNE WELLINGTON
CAPE TOWN SALISBURY IBADAN NAIROBI LUSAKA ADDIS ABABA
BOMBAY CALCUTTA MADRAS KARACHI LAHORE DACCA
KUALA LUMPUR HONG KONG TOKYO

*Printed in Great Britain by*
*Western Printing Services Ltd., Bristol*

# FOREWORD

*by* PHILIP MASON

*Director, Institute of Race Relations*

ONE of the difficulties in obtaining reliable information about immigrants is that it is not easy to obtain a random sample; it would be unsafe to generalize from samples taken at place of residence or work because friends tend to help each other to find work and houses and so there is clustering of people with similar backgrounds. Dr. Davison came to the Institute with an ingenious proposal for overcoming this difficulty for one group, Jamaicans; he would begin at the Jamaican end and, on certain days chosen at random, take for his sample anyone claiming a passport the number of which contained a certain figure. People so selected would be interviewed in Jamaica and as far as possible would be traced on arrival in Britain and their history recorded. To the material thus obtained were subsequently added figures extracted by computer from the 1961 Census material in respect of London only, but relating to all Commonwealth immigrants and not only to Jamaicans.

Statistics about immigrants and race in Britain are notoriously subject to uncertainty and are likely to remain so unless we adopt racial definitions, a course to which there are obvious objections. Dr. Davison's work could not possibly end this uncertainty and does, like all statistical work on immigrants at present, involve elements of conjecture and deduction. These he has stated. His figures will no doubt be criticized, as most published figures have been; I suspect that in most cases the criticisms will make little difference to the trends revealed or at any rate suggested. These are interesting and some of them important.

For example, the size of families in London shows only a slight range of difference for heads of households born in Poland, England, Pakistan and India, between 2·67 per household for Poland and 2·79 for India; for Ireland the average is 3·18, for Jamaica 3·28 and for Cyprus 4·23. For overcrowding, one set of figures concerns the percentage of people living at a density of more than 1·5 persons per room. This applies to 8% only of persons living in households of which the head was born in England; 9% of which the head was born in Poland; 24% India; 29% Pakistan; 32% Ireland; 41% Cyprus; 53% Jamaica; 63% rest of Caribbean. Then there are figures about access to various facilities. Of English families, defined as above, 55% have exclusive use of hot-water tap; they are beaten in this by India 65%, Poland 63%, Pakistan 60%; for families with heads from Cyprus the corresponding figure is 44%, Ireland 38%, Jamaica 21% and the rest of the Caribbean 19%. Dr. Davison finds the high position of Indians and Pakistanis in this list surprising, but to anyone who has lived in the Indian sub-continent it will suggest that Indians and Pakistanis have brought with them their intense regard for personal cleanliness and put hot water at the top of their priorities.

The pattern of housing for immigrants is quite different from that of the English, 53% of whom rent unfurnished rooms while 24% have rented council houses and 13% are owner-occupiers. This is in contrast with Poles and Cypriots, for both of whom the pattern is about one-third owner-occupiers and one-third renting unfurnished. Of Indians, 48% rent furnished and 26% unfurnished while 16% are owner-occupiers, and Pakistanis are not very different. But 61% of Jamaicans and 75% of other Caribbeans live in furnished rooms, while 25% of Jamaicans are owner-occupiers. Broadly speaking, council houses and unfurnished rooms are for natives, while for immigrants it is a matter of furnished rooms until enough money can be scraped together for a house.

Of the English, 66% of males and 39% of females are economically active. For Jamaicans, the corresponding figures are 88% and 62%. The English have the lowest figure for economically active males, Pakistan for females—31%. Indian females are placed surprisingly high at 48%. So much for the belief that 'these people come over here to live on us'. The figures for kinds of employment are less revealing than might have been hoped, but they suggest a trend by Poles, Cypriots and Indians to form small independent businesses which is not followed by Irish, Jamaicans or other Caribbeans. Ireland, Jamaica and the rest of the Caribbean provide the highest percentages of unskilled and semi-skilled manual labour. Unemployment figures for immigrants are consistently above the national average for the period quoted, but on the whole the gap has been steadily reduced; for November 1964 the national average was 1·5%, while for Commonwealth immigrants the averages were: male, 2·0%, female 3·4%. These figures do not touch on suitability of employment to qualifications held.

All the points above are based on Census figures for London, and Birmingham or Bradford might show different trends. The random sample for Jamaicans covers the whole of the United Kingdom and concerns rather different aspects of the immigrants' life. The use made of labour exchanges is low, and lower in the second year than the first. About 70% of jobs found (for men and women) are through a friend or by casual application (about equally divided) and this trend is slightly more marked in the second year. Colour discrimination while at work was alleged in only five out of 216 interviews. The income of Jamaican households was well below the national average for unskilled workers, both for men and women; between 9% and 16% of earnings are sent back to Jamaica. In the first year, 74% of men and 86% of women said they meant to go back to Jamaica one day; in the second year, the corresponding figures were 81% and 89%. But only 26% of men and 16% of women had saved any money for the return. On the other hand, questioning as to how problems of housing, employment, and accommodation with neighbours were being solved showed a surprisingly high degree of success.

These seem to me the main trends which emerge and they are of value to everyone interested in the subject. We are very grateful to the Joseph Rowntree Memorial Trust for making Dr. Davison's researches possible.

# PREFACE

By inviting me early in 1961 to join the West Indies Commission in London as an Adviser, the Hon. N. W. Manley, Q.C., then Premier of Jamaica, made the present project possible. A year later Sir Alexander Bustamante extended the invitation to remain for a further year as Adviser to the Jamaican High Commission. Mr Philip Mason, Director of the Institute of Race Relations, was instrumental in securing the grant to meet the cost of the fieldwork from the Joseph Rowntree Memorial Trust and the then Vice-Chancellor of the University of the West Indies, Professor W. A. Lewis, permitted me to undertake the work by releasing me from my duties in the University on secondment to the Government of Jamaica. Many volunteers, listed in Appendix A, responded generously to a request that they should visit Jamaican migrants at home. No less important was the ready response from the Jamaican migrants themselves, who willingly responded in almost every case to requests for personal details, often of a delicate nature. The extent to which this information was given freely and usually frankly was an encouraging sign that, given the right approach, whatever problems of race relations may exist in Britain today they are by no means insurmountable. The migrants themselves were promised anonymity.

The Census data were analysed on a computer operated by the Royal Army Pay Corps at Worthy Down. At the time that the present project was initiated the G.R.O. had no plans for publishing separate statistics relating to Commonwealth immigrants as such, although such tables have now been prepared. The practical assistance given by Mr. R. T. Thorby of the General Register Office of England and Wales in collaborating in the production of the particular statistical analyses required for this work is gratefully acknowledged. The cost of writing the programme for the computer and extracting the data from the magnetic tapes was met from the Rowntree grant. Out of the mass of information obtained only highly condensed tables (for which the author accepts responsibility) have been used in this book.

Without the successful interviews originally conducted in the

Kingston passport office by Mrs. Betty Davison the project could not have been launched at all. She continued in London to visit migrants throughout the term of the enquiry and to keep in touch with the many voluntary visitors while employed as the project secretary and research worker by the Institute of Race Relations. The first eight chapters of this book have been written by the undersigned; the last one, 'Flight to Disenchantment', has been written as a series of individual case studies by Betty Davison, and is based upon tape-recorded interviews taken in the London homes of people she first met in the Kingston passport office.

I should also like to record my thanks to the members of the administrative, clerical and library staff of the Institute of Race Relations who have been unfailingly helpful to me throughout this project.

Whilst so many people have co-operated in the production of this book it will be understood that the responsibility for any statistics or interpretations of the statistics must rest on the author alone.

R. B. DAVISON
*University of the West Indies,*
*Mona, Kingston, Jamaica,*
*August 1965*

# CONTENTS

# LIST OF TABLES

NOTE: In a number of tables using percentages the process of rounding off to the nearest whole number in the constituent items means that the totals do not always exactly equal 100.

# Chapter I

## BACKGROUND

THE Commonwealth Immigrants Act reached the United Kingdom statute book early in 1962 at the end of a violent political controversy. The Act came into force fully on 1 July 1962. On that date all Commonwealth citizens except, broadly speaking, those born in the United Kingdom or holding United Kingdom passports, came under new regulations regarding immigration and, a month previously, new penalties regarding deportation.

During the second reading of the Commonwealth Immigrants Bill in the House of Commons, the then Home Secretary, Mr. R. A. Butler, was subjected to a certain amount of criticism because of the alleged inadequacy of the statistics which he presented to the House regarding the overall migration into and out of Britain. The substance of the criticism was in some respects justified, for it was clear that the Bill had been introduced in haste without a fully adequate examination of the statistical argument upon which it had been based. This was that immigration, particularly coloured immigration, had reached an excessive level. On the other hand it was hardly fair to accuse the Government of default for not presenting statistics which they, at that time, had no statutory power to collect. Until the new Act came into force on 1 July 1962, the United Kingdom authorities possessed the power to examine the passport of a Commonwealth citizen entering the country only in order to satisfy themselves that he or she was, in fact, a Commonwealth citizen. They had no statutory powers to keep records of British subjects entering or leaving Britain. Nevertheless for a number of years the Home Office had, in fact, attempted to keep some sort of estimate of numbers of Commonwealth citizens arriving in and leaving Britain. As these figures were based not on any record card completed by the travellers, but on counts made by immigration officers, often working under some pressure, they were necessarily estimates, not precise figures. There is nevertheless no reason to doubt that they are substantially correct, and a comparison of the inward and

outward flow yields a reliable estimate of the net inward movement over the six years preceding the imposition of controls.

The Home Secretary periodically gave a summary of the
estimates in reply to questions in the House of Commons, but
the complete figures had never been published in one place.
The Home Office were good enough to collect the relevant
statistics together in one table, and gave permission for them to
be published.[1] These figures relate to what may be called the
'tropical Commonwealth' and do not cover the 'temperate
Commonwealth'—Australia, New Zealand, Canada and Cen-
tral Africa. South Africa is also excluded. British Guiana and
British Honduras are included with the West Indies. Table
1(a) has been carried forward to 30 June 1962, when the new
Act came into force. From 1 July a new set of statistics began to
appear based upon the administration of the new Act, and they
are not therefore strictly comparable with the estimates now
under review.

If we examine the record of immigration from the tropical
Commonwealth since 1955 (Table 1(b)), we can first of all
observe that it does not show a steadily rising trend. If we take
1955 = 100, the numbers increased by 10% in the following
year and then fell year after year until by 1959 the index was
84—a fall of nearly 20% from 1955. Then the index number
rose sharply to 153 in 1960 and again to 262 in 1961. It was
this sudden, sharp rise which prompted the Government to
introduce the Commonwealth Immigrants Act. When we look
at the outgoing figures a totally different situation emerges.
Here we have almost a continuous rise from 1955 to 1961. The
numbers leaving the country in 1961 were almost double those
of 1955. This fact was certainly not clearly brought out at any
stage during the debate on the Bill in the House of Commons.

When, as in Table 2, we examine the territories from which
these 'tropical Commonwealth' immigrants originated, we
find some quite striking differences. Over the whole period just
over one-third of the immigrants (38%) came from the West
Indies, and just under a quarter (23%) from Jamaica. But only
one in ten of the departures (12%) went back to the islands. In
consequence the West Indies provided just over half (56%) of

---

[1] The statistics used in the earlier part of this chapter were first published and
discussed in an article by the present author in the *British Journal of Industrial Relations*, Vol. I, No. 1, pp. 43–61.

## TABLE I (a)

### Estimate of Movement into and out of the United Kingdom of Persons from the Tropical Commonwealth, 1955 to 30 June 1962

| | 1955 | | | 1956 | | | 1957 | | | 1958 | | |
|---|---|---|---|---|---|---|---|---|---|---|---|---|
| | In | Out | Net inward | In | Out | Net inward | In | Out | Net inward | In | Out | Net inward |
| Jamaica | NA | NA | NA | 19,800 | 2,200 | 17,600 | 14,020 | 2,700 | 11,320 | 11,500 | 3,490 | 8,010 |
| Rest of West Indies | NA | NA | NA | 13,600 | 1,400 | 12,200 | 13,600 | 1,900 | 11,700 | 9,210 | 2,200 | 7,010 |
| Total of West Indies | 30,370 | 2,820 | 27,550 | | | | | | | | | |
| India | 18,470 | 12,670 | 5,800 | 20,000 | 14,400 | 5,600 | 20,160 | 13,540 | 6,620 | 17,140 | 10,940 | 6,200 |
| Pakistan | 8,170 | 6,320 | 1,850 | 9,030 | 6,980 | 2,050 | 11,820 | 6,650 | 5,170 | 10,160 | 5,490 | 4,690 |
| Cyprus | 6,310 | 2,860 | 3,450 | 5,110 | 2,340 | 2,770 | 3,960 | 2,510 | 1,450 | 5,640 | 2,920 | 2,720 |
| West Africa | 4,160 | 2,650 | 1,510 | 4,870 | 2,890 | 1,980 | 5,520 | 3,320 | 2,200 | 4,780 | 3,820 | 960 |
| East Africa | 1,680 | 990 | 690 | 1,630 | 950 | 680 | 1,890 | 1,260 | 630 | 1,590 | 1,170 | 420 |
| Hong Kong | 800 | 500 | 300 | 1,210 | 660 | 550 | 1,600 | 710 | 890 | 1,370 | 1,170 | 200 |
| Others | 6,190 | 4,640 | 1,550 | 9,530 | 6,110 | 3,420 | 8,180 | 5,760 | 2,420 | 6,480 | 6,790 | −310 |
| TOTAL | 76,150 | 33,450 | 42,700 | 84,780 | 37,930 | 46,850 | 80,750 | 38,350 | 42,400 | 67,890 | 37,990 | 29,900 |

| | 1959 | | | 1960 | | | 1961 | | | 1962 First six months only | | |
|---|---|---|---|---|---|---|---|---|---|---|---|---|
| | In | Out | Net inward | In | Out | Net inward | In | Out | Net inward | In | Out | Net inward |
| Jamaica | 13,700 | 3,410 | 10,290 | 35,840 | 4,430 | 31,410 | 45,220 | 4,540 | 40,680 | 24,190 | 2,420 | 21,770 |
| Rest of West Indies | 8,690 | 2,590 | 6,100 | 21,330 | 3,070 | 18,260 | 29,370 | 3,760 | 25,610 | 12,050 | 2,020 | 10,030 |
| Total of West Indies | | | | | | | | | | | | |
| India | 15,450 | 12,520 | 2,930 | 22,170 | 16,250 | 5,920 | 39,930 | 16,180 | 23,750 | 25,650 | 6,600 | 19,050 |
| Pakistan | 6,780 | 5,920 | 860 | 9,850 | 7,350 | 2,500 | 33,640 | 8,550 | 25,080 | 28,940 | 3,850 | 25,090 |
| Cyprus | 3,750 | 3,350 | 400 | 7,740 | 4,540 | 3,200 | 12,300 | 5,440 | 6,860 | 6,640 | 3,480 | 3,160 |
| West Africa | 5,860 | 5,100 | 760 | 7,580 | 8,070 | −490 | 15,550 | 10,100 | 5,450 | 11,000 | 4,040 | 6,960 |
| East Africa | 1,350 | 1,230 | 120 | 1,960 | 1,710 | 250 | 4,270 | 1,610 | 2,660 | 2,920 | 940 | 1,980 |
| Hong Kong | 1,570 | 1,120 | 450 | 2,370 | 1,860 | 510 | 3,750 | 1,600 | 2,150 | 3,120 | 970 | 2,150 |
| Others | 6,960 | 7,270 | −310 | 7,660 | 11,520 | −3,860 | 15,520 | 11,360 | 4,160 | 9,940 | 5,240 | 4,700 |
| TOTAL | 64,110 | 42,510 | 21,600 | 116,500 | 58,800 | 57,700 | 199,550 | 63,150 | 136,400 | 124,450 | 29,560 | 94,890 |

*Source:* Home Office

((1) A minus sign denotes a net *outward* movement. (2) NA means 'not available'. (3) The 'tropical Commonwealth' includes all Commonwealth countries other than the United Kingdom, Canada, Australia, New Zealand, and the Federation of Rhodesia and Nyasaland. South Africa is also excluded.)

## TABLE I (b)

### Index of Movements between the United Kingdom and the Tropical Commonwealth, 1955 to 30 June 1962

| Year | Index In | Out | Net inward |
|---|---|---|---|
| 1955 | 100 | 100 | 100 |
| 1956 | 111 | 113 | 110 |
| 1957 | 106 | 115 | 99 |
| 1958 | 89 | 114 | 70 |
| 1959 | 84 | 127 | 51 |
| 1960 | 153 | 176 | 135 |
| 1961 | 262 | 189 | 319 |

the total net inward movement. India provided just under a quarter of the intake (22%) but almost a third (31%) of the outflow. Her contribution to the net inflow was therefore only 16%, only slightly higher than Pakistan, which provided 14%. It is clear that so far as India and Pakistan are concerned, the migration was much more a two-way stream than was the case with the rest of the tropical Commonwealth.

## TABLE 2

### Estimated Movement between the United Kingdom and the Tropical Commonwealth, by Territory of Origin, 1955–62

| Territory of origin | In per cent | Out per cent | Net inward per cent |
|---|---|---|---|
| Jamaica | 23 | 7 | 34 |
| Rest of West Indies | 15 | 5 | 22 |
| Total West Indies | 38 | 12 | 56 |
| India | 22 | 31 | 16 |
| Pakistan | 14 | 15 | 14 |
| West Africa | 7 | 12 | 4 |
| East Africa | 2 | 3 | 1 |
| Total Tropical Africa | 9 | 15 | 5 |
| Cyprus | 6 | 8 | 5 |
| Hong Kong | 2 | 2 | 2 |
| Others | 9 | 17 | 2 |
| | 100 | 100 | 100 |

*Source:* Home Office

We can compare these results with the estimates made by the *Economist* Intelligence Unit of the net immigration into Britain in the years 1946–59.[1] They are not strictly comparable because they cover a different period and have been prepared on a different (but not clearly specified) basis. The West Indian figure tallies almost exactly. The Home Office says that 56% of the net immigrants came from that area; the *Economist* says 54%. The figures for India and Pakistan, however, are significantly different (Home Office 30%, *Economist* 21%). The experience since July 1962 is recorded in Table 3.

TABLE 3

*Admissions, Embarkations and Net Inflow into the United Kingdom of Persons subject to the Commonwealth Immigrants Act, 1962*

| Quarter | | Admissions | Embarkations | Net balance |
|---|---|---|---|---|
| 1962 | July–Sept. | 129,001 | 122,953 | + 6,048 |
| | Oct.–Dec. | 54,415 | 57,960 | − 3,545 |
| 1963 | Jan.–Mar. | 48,585 | 40,189 | + 8,396 |
| | Apr.–June | 101,242 | 77,618 | +28,624 |
| | July–Sept. | 147,582 | 123,465 | +24,117 |
| | Oct.–Dec. | 68,328 | 58,465 | + 9,863 |
| 1964 | Jan.–Mar. | 56,604 | 40,122 | +16,482 |
| | Apr.–June | 113,173 | 80,500 | +32,673 |
| | July–Sept. | 163,713 | 143,061 | +20,652 |
| | Oct.–Dec. | 73,111 | 67,419 | + 5,692 |
| 1965 | Jan.–Mar. | 63,591 | 44,308 | +19,283 |
| | Apr.–June | 125,798 | 95,984 | +19,814 |
| | July–Sept. | 172,376 | 157,242 | +15,134 |

*Source:* Home Office

It was against the background of rising numbers of immigrants recorded in Table 1(a) that in 1960 concern was being expressed in many quarters in Britain at the possibility of increasing racial tension in Britain. The street disturbances in Nottingham and Notting Hill in September 1958 had focused public attention on the issue, although the official policy of the British Government was that the best way to deal with the problems that were arising was to leave them alone in the belief that the problems would solve themselves in time. Not until the then Home Secretary announced to the Conservative Party

[1] 'Studies on Immigration from the Commonwealth: (1) Basic Statistics', London, *Economist* Intelligence Unit, 1962.

Conference in October 1961 that legislation was pending to control Commonwealth immigration, was there any public recognition by the British Government that there was any problem at all. Its dimensions were certainly unknown, since very little statistical information on the question of coloured immigrants in Britain was available in 1961. No one knew with any certainty, for instance, how many Commonwealth immigrants had entered and left the country since the 1951 Census or where they were settled in Britain. Statistics on any other aspect of the life of the immigrants were virtually unobtainable, and practical policies of social welfare agencies had to be based mainly on guesswork, supplemented by a very limited amount of published work, largely based on case studies, rather than any kind of comprehensive statistical analyses.

*Coloured Immigrants in Britain*, a survey by the Institute of Race Relations published in 1960, was designed, in the words of its foreword, 'to collect what facts were known and put them together'. The facts proved to be, in many cases, conspicuous by their absence, although the Institute survey performed a most useful service by filling in many gaps by reasoned estimates.

Towards the latter end of 1960, following the publication of *Coloured Immigrants in Britain*, preliminary discussions took place in the Institute as to how the survey work reported in that book could best be followed up. Independently, in March 1961 a paper was circulated within the Social Science Faculty of the University College (now University) of the West Indies in Jamaica,[1] which drew attention to the then recent increase in the numbers of West Indian migrants to Britain and the rising political pressures in Britain concerning the question of racial tension and possible immigration control. This paper proposed the launching of a new research project in this field. It was pointed out that a census had recently been taken in the West Indies, and within a week or two (in April 1961) one would also be taken in Britain which opened the way for an academic approach to the subject on lines which had not been possible before. Previous work in the subject could be divided into two groups—that conducted in the West Indies, and that conducted in Britain. There had never been an attempt to conduct related

---

[1] R. B. Davison, 'West Indian Migration to Britain, Memorandum on Research' (unpublished cyclostyled report in the Department of Economics), University of the West Indies, 1961.

research from both the sending and receiving end of the migration. In the West Indies the study by Maunder[1] had been a useful pioneer effort but was already several years out of date. It was conducted with two small samples only and the interviews were, inevitably, brief. The study by Roberts and Mills[2] was scholarly and exhaustive in its field. It was based on a study of embarkation cards collected by the Government of Jamaica and provided much useful information, but had not involved any interviewing of the migrants by social workers. Reubens[3] was currently at work on a study of inter-island migration in the West Indies. The results were not then available but have since been published.

In the United Kingdom extremely valuable work had been done by sociologists, particularly those connected with the University of Edinburgh, but they had tended to concentrate largely on 'problem' residential areas[4] using an intensive case-study social anthropology approach almost exclusively. One study edited by Ruck[5] had contained general information contributed by several authors, and was largely based on an analysis of enquiries made by Citizens' Advice Bureaux and casework offices. It was, therefore, primarily a study of the problems of immigrants, taking no account of the vast majority who did not need to resort to any social welfare agencies at all. Mrs. Ruth Glass[6] had used records collected in the Migrant Services Division of the West Indies Commission but had apparently not followed this up by any form of interviewing amongst the migrants themselves on a systematic basis. At that time the work of Mrs. Sheila Patterson[7] had not yet appeared. Valuable though all these contributions had been it was

[1] W. F. Maunder, 'The New Jamaican Emigration', *Social and Economic Studies*, Vol. IV, No. 1, 1955, p. 38.

[2] G. W. Roberts and D. O. Mills, 'Study of External Migration affecting Jamaica: 1953–5', *Social and Economic Studies*, Vol. VII, No. 2 (supplement, June 1958).

[3] F. P. Reubens, 'Migration and Development in the West Indies', *Studies in Federal Economics*, No. 3, U.C.W.I., 1962.

[4] For instance, A. H. Richmond, *Colour Prejudice in Britain*, London, Routledge and Kegan Paul, 1954; M. Banton, *White and Coloured*, London, Cape, 1959.

[5] S. K. Ruck (ed.), *The West Indian Comes to England* (a report for the Trustees of the London Parochial Charities by the Family Welfare Association), London, Routledge, 1960.

[6] Ruth Glass, *Newcomers: the West Indians in London*, London, Allen and Unwin, 1960.

[7] S. Patterson, *Dark Strangers*, London, Tavistock Publications, 1963.

proposed that a different approach was worth considering which would not rely at all upon using any kind of social welfare agency—which must import a serious bias into any form of sampling, simply because such agencies exist primarily for dealing with problems—to draw the initial sample or make the contacts with persons to be interviewed. Several lines of approach were canvassed but it was finally suggested that the best way to draw a sample was by conducting interviews in the Kingston Passport Office in Jamaica. All migrants to Britain need to have a passport, all of which are issued from one office in Jamaica. To take a random sample from passport applicants there presented the nearest practical approach to an unbiased sampling procedure which could be devised. With the aid of funds provided by the Institute of Social and Economic Research in the University of the West Indies, this project was successfully launched and completed by June 1961. The results of the enquiries in Jamaica and the method of conducting the survey have already been published.[1] Briefly the method was to mark every tenth passport, by random choice of numbers, and interview the person to whom it was issued in the Passport Office itself. One of the main objects of this phase of the project was to discover, where possible, the precise address to which the migrant intended to travel in Britain and these addresses were obtained from 55% of the men and 84% of the women out of a total number of 364 in the sample. As a result of further enquiries in Jamaica with the aid of school teachers all over the island other addresses were subsequently obtained.

Meanwhile arrangements had been made by the Institute of Race Relations with the Joseph Rowntree Memorial Trust to launch a new programme of research in race relations and it was agreed that the follow-up of the sample already obtained in Jamaica should be incorporated as one of the projects in this programme. The main object was to follow up as many as possible of the people interviewed in the original sample, wherever they could be located in Britain over as long a period of time as possible, with the aid of social workers selected from voluntary agencies and/or public authorities with experience of work amongst coloured immigrants.

[1] R. B. Davison, *West Indian Migrants*, London, Oxford University Press for the Institute of Race Relations, 1962.

During the original enquiry in Jamaica, approximately 5 %[1] of the total number of persons for whom passports were prepared in the period of the survey were interviewed and classified as potential migrants to Britain. By correspondence and personal visits 272 persons (75 % of the original sample) were contacted later in England and supplied useful information. No contact was made with the remaining ninety-two persons, but it was found by enquiries in England and in Jamaica that twenty-two of them had never left Jamaica, one had died, one had joined the army, one was a student, one had gone back to Jamaica and one was too seriously ill to be interviewed. Thus a further 7 % of the sample was accounted for. Of the remainder, twenty-eight were not known at all at the United Kingdom addresses they had originally given in Jamaica, a further seventeen were known at the addresses given, but had moved away before our interviewer arrived without notifying any change of address to us or, apparently, to anyone else. This group amounted to 12 % of the sample. Of the remaining 6 % no trace was ever found anywhere, in Jamaica or Britain, and no explanation can be offered regarding their disappearance. It is quite possible that some of them (and some of those who were not known at the United Kingdom address supplied) never left Jamaica at all.

All the interviews were conducted with the aid of standard questionnaires provided with space for personal comments, but it was felt that a valuable contribution could also be made by studying in depth a few individual cases selected from the sample. In these cases the open-ended interviews followed the standardized questionnaire.[2] Out of the twenty detailed case studies completed in this way five have been selected to form the final chapter of this book, which has been written by Mrs. Betty Davison.

This survey was confined to one migrant group only—the Jamaicans—and as time and resources were limited, could only relate to a fairly small sample. It was realized that this particular

---

[1] Although one passport in ten was marked as produced, not all of the passports were collected during the period of the interviewing and also some of those interviewed were not regarded as 'migrants' to Britain, as they proved to be temporary visitors, under age, or not going to Britain at all. These categories were therefore excluded from the survey.

[2] The questionnaire was modified during the second year of the study. The final version is reproduced in Appendix B.

enquiry would greatly benefit if it could be amplified by making use of some of the data collected during the Census of England and Wales which had been taken in April 1961. Discussions therefore took place with the Census Branch of the General Register Office for England and Wales, which was engaged upon processing the Census data with the aid of an electronic computer, and arrangements were made to use the computer for the purpose of extracting data relating to Jamaicans and several other immigrant groups by means of a separate and special tabulation. It was not possible to study separately all the immigrant groups which can be identified in the United Kingdom population and eight groups were in fact selected. Jamaicans were clearly the first group listed as they were the main focus of the study, and then 'Caribbeans' were the obvious second choice. The organization of the data inside the computer would have permitted separate identification of the various islands and territories in the Caribbean area, other than Jamaica, but these have been treated as one unit and the blanket term 'Caribbean' is used throughout the present study to include people from the Commonwealth territories in the Caribbean area, apart from Jamaica.[1] Comparison with other coloured immigrants from a different part of the Commonwealth was felt to be desirable, and, as the numbers of migrants from India and Pakistan to Britain were then beginning to increase sharply, and at the time of writing provide the bulk of the inflow from the tropical Commonwealth into Britain, these two countries were next selected. One problem—which must apply in the Census generally—was that people now migrating from Pakistan were born in British India. When asked to state their birthplace, such people could rightly say 'India', but they are today citizens of Pakistan. There was no solution for this difficulty—it may safely be assumed, however, that if any degree of error has arisen in the general Census tables over this point, an error of similar magnitude occurs in this study. Another Commonwealth territory which has provided a noticeable proportion of recent migrants to Britain is Cyprus. Such immigrants may not have a 'colour' problem as such, but they do have a language problem and it was decided to use the Cypriot group also for comparative purposes.

[1] These include British Guiana, British Honduras, Trinidad and Tobago, Barbados, the Leeward Islands, the Windward Islands and the British Virgin Islands.

A good deal of discussion has taken place as to whether the social problems reported amongst coloured immigrants are due to the fact that they are 'coloured' or 'immigrants' or both. Accordingly the next two groups selected were immigrants, but not coloured immigrants. The Poles are a minority group, many of whom were left stranded in Britain at the end of the second World War, choosing to stay in Britain rather than return to a Communist Poland. They initially had a language problem but it was felt that it would be interesting to see how far, after the lapse of some twenty years, they approximate in their housing position, for instance, to other immigrant groups and to the native English. The Irish have neither a colour problem nor a language problem—but they have an historical problem when they migrate to Britain, and the Irish were therefore selected as the seventh immigrant group.[1]

It would have been possible, once the tabulations had been received from the computer, to set the recorded experience of each of these immigrant groups in juxtaposition, not only with each other but also with the recorded experience of the British population as a whole. This information can be obtained from the published Census tables[2] and is undoubtedly a useful comparison to make but it has the serious disadvantage that the aggregate figure for the population as a whole itself contains the experience of the various immigrant groups. Accordingly a random sample of one in twenty-five of the heads of households born in England was taken, specifically for this purpose, by the Census Office computer. This group, rather than the population as a whole, is then used as a kind of baseline in the following analysis when comparing immigrant groups one with the other, and with the host population.

During the Census the full range of questions was answered by 10% of the population and a shorter list by the remaining 90%. No Census tables had been published when the present study began, and it soon became clear that unless the completion of the project was to be unduly delayed it would be necessary to confine attention to the London area as defined in the London County Report—that is to say the twenty-eight metropolitan boroughs. Statistics were also obtained for the

[1] Compare, for example, S. Patterson, 'Polish London', and J. A. Jackson, 'The Irish', in *London: Aspects of Change*, London, MacGibbon and Kee, 1964.
[2] *Census 1961: England and Wales—County Report*, London, H.M.S.O.

City of London which is included in the County of London, but they have not been used in this study in view of the fact that the City, being primarily a commercial centre, has peculiar residential characteristics. The mass of data to be analysed (over three million records) meant that whilst the whole of London could be included in this study so far as the 10% sample was concerned, only selected boroughs could be used in the case of the 90% of the population which completed the shortened version of the Census schedule. Again keeping the primary focus on Jamaicans, seven boroughs were therefore selected which showed the largest proportion of Jamaicans in the borough population, namely Lambeth, Stoke Newington, Hackney, Battersea, Deptford, Camberwell and Paddington.[1] In each of these boroughs the computer extracted details of every household which had a person born in one of the selected overseas territories recorded first on the Census schedule. In the case of persons born in England all the records were examined but details were extracted on the basis of a random sample of one household in twenty-five. It was realized at the outset that the selection of seven boroughs in London could not yield a valid basis for confident generalizations relating to London as a whole and certainly not for the rest of the United Kingdom. Nevertheless, working on the principle that an approximate result based on even an imperfect sample is preferable to no information at all, the work proceeded on this basis in the hope that perhaps one day the facilities will be available for a more exhaustive analysis based on samples drawn from the whole of Britain.

If the head of a household (who was assumed to be the first person listed in the household, male or female) had recorded a birthplace in one of the seven selected overseas countries, the computer extracted the information relating to the individuals resident in the whole of that household. The same procedure was followed, on a one-in-twenty-five sampling basis, for those households where the head was born in England. This method of selection implies that in the case of mixed marriages (where the wife or consort was not born in the same territory as her husband) she is, in effect, regarded as having the same birthplace as her husband. Furthermore all the children of the

[1] For further discussion on immigrant groups in London, see 'The Distribution of Immigrant Groups in London', *Race*, Vol. V, No. 2, October 1963.

household—whether born in England or not—are similarly regarded as, say, 'Jamaicans' if the head of the household in which they were living was born in Jamaica. By adopting this procedure it is possible to examine the structure of households and their housing accommodation more realistically than if individuals only had been selected. However, the questions answered by the 10% of the population which relate to occupation, industry, workplace, educational terminal age and residence changes are better considered on an individual basis, and in these cases the computer extracted data strictly on the basis of the birthplace of the individual.

The information relating to the various immigrant categories was processed according to the identical computer programme which is being used for the Census generally. This means that the statistics prepared for each group in each borough can be compared one with the other and with the general Census tables. In the tables which appear in the following text where information has been derived from the seven boroughs covering 100% of the population the source is indicated as the 'full Census analysis'. Where the statistics have been derived from all the twenty-eight metropolitan boroughs covering 10% of the population only, the source is indicated as the '10% Census analysis'. The remaining tables have been derived from the questionnaires completed during the field survey of the random sample of Jamaican migrants and are indicated in the source as 'Jamaican Sample Survey'. It should be clear from the context which part of the commentary relates to a particular table.

The method of selecting the samples from the full Census returns of the seven boroughs, which was based on households, not individuals, meant that a proportion of the persons in the selected households were not born in the same country as the head of the household. In the following table the ascertainable facts recorded in this connection are summarized. The computer, in this case, included Jamaicans along with other Caribbeans in one category.

There was also a single category for India, Pakistan and Ceylon. As we were concerned only with households the heads of which were born in India and Pakistan, but not Ceylon, a minor but unavoidable error may have crept into these statistics. It is likely to be very small and may safely be ignored. This table shows separately for males and females the number

TABLE 4

*Birthplace Groups in Seven London Boroughs*

| Birthplace of head of household* | Number of households | Number of persons living in those households | Per cent of persons Born in same country as head of the household | Born in U.K. |
|---|---|---|---|---|
| (a) MALES | | | | |
| England | 9,604§ | 12,438§ | — | 94 |
| British Caribbean† | 12,808 | 21,056 | 81 | 18 |
| India, Pakistan | 2,459 | 3,726 | 75 | 21 |
| Poland | 3,793 | 5,183 | 66‖ | 30 |
| Ireland‡ | 13,914 | 22,410 | 64 | 35 |
| Cyprus | 1,891 | 4,194 | 74 | 24 |
| (b) FEMALES | | | | |
| England | 9,604§ | 13,850§ | — | 97 |
| British Caribbean† | 12,808 | 18,780 | 74 | 24 |
| India, Pakistan | 2,459 | 3,144 | 51 | 38 |
| Poland | 3,793 | 4,953 | 49‖ | 47 |
| Ireland | 13,914 | 21,858 | 54 | 44 |
| Cyprus | 1,891 | 3,819 | 63 | 31 |

*Source:* full Census analysis, 1961

\* The first person listed on the household, male or female, is assumed throughout to be the head of the household.

† Including Jamaica.

‡ Northern Ireland and the Republic of Ireland.

§ 1 in 25 sample.

‖ The computer programme did not distinguish between 'Poland' and 'foreign areas'. It is reasonable to assume that the great majority of persons living in Polish households who were born in 'foreign areas' were in fact born in Poland.

of households included in each of the selected birthplace groups, the number of persons living in those households and the proportion of persons who were born in the same country as the head of the household and the proportion born in the United Kingdom.

The great majority of persons living in a household headed by a person born in England were themselves born in the United Kingdom. The proportion is 94% of the males and 97% of the females. Clearly there is no evidence here that English-born persons are marrying immigrants to any noticeable extent. Amongst the immigrant households the proportion of persons born in the same country as the heads of the households is much lower, but the proportion born in the United Kingdom varies considerably. In the British Caribbean group 81 % of the males and 74% of the females were born in the British Caribbean. Almost all the others were born in the United Kingdom. It was, unfortunately, not possible to analyse the figures sufficiently finely on this occasion to decide how many of the 24% of the females born in the United Kingdom were adults and how many were children born of parents both of whom came from the British Caribbean area. There is no technical reason why this could not be done on some future occasion but pressure of work on the computer prevented this line of enquiry from being pursued in connection with the present study. Not far short of half the females (44% to 47%) recorded in households headed by a person born in Poland or Ireland were born in the United Kingdom.

This discussion of the methodology of the survey should make it clear that no claim is being advanced that it has been a comprehensive study of the entire field. On the contrary it has been recognized from the beginning of the project that a great deal more work needs to be done. The Jamaican sample survey relates only to one immigrant group. Useful comparative studies could be made of other immigrant groups and it may well be found that the experience of the Jamaicans is very different from that of the Pakistanis, Indians, Cypriots and others not mentioned specifically in this book. It may be doubted if any useful purpose would be served by extending the London Census analysis of the selected household groups beyond the seven boroughs considered here, for the variation between the boroughs is quite small in most cases, but it would certainly be worth while if similar information could be obtained relating to a number of provincial cities where a very different picture may emerge from that which appears in London.

Since this project was first mooted there have been considerable changes both in public policies and public attitudes towards the whole question of immigrants in England and a great deal of additional information is now available. Up to the time when the decision to enact the Commonwealth Immigrants Act was first made public, the general official policy of the British Government, at least in its public manifestation, was to ignore completely the whole subject of Commonwealth immigration and race relations in general in Britain. Even people who engaged in research in such matters, and certainly those who attempted openly to recognize the potentiality of racial conflict in Britain whilst urging that some positive steps should be taken officially to deal with it, were usually discouraged by officials and private citizens in general, as it was felt that the open discussion of questions of race relations might only lead to an intensification of the problems involved. All this is changed at the time of writing. In the Queen's Speech of November 1964, immediately upon taking office, the new British Labour Government announced that legislation was pending to deal with a number of aspects of racial discrimination in Britain although control of Commonwealth immigration was to continue. Following the return of the Mountbatten mission to the various Commonwealth countries principally concerned, a White Paper was published[1] by the Labour Government (the Labour Party having completely reversed its policy on immigration after 1962) which indicated a severe curtailment of further immigration from the Commonwealth into Britain whilst promising a considerable development, backed by financial provisions, in the positive programmes designed to facilitate the integration of coloured immigrants into the British community. Such practical policies can only be usefully developed if they rest on a basis of objective analysis of the facts of the existing situation. If the present project makes even the slightest contribution towards the development of sound policies in this field, the time, money and effort spent upon it will have been well worth while.

[1] 'Immigration from the Commonwealth', Cmnd. 2739, London, H.M.S.O., August 1965.

## Chapter II

## THE IMMIGRANT POPULATION
## OF LONDON

THE last British Census, taken in April 1961, was intended to enumerate household by household everyone in the country at midnight on Sunday, 23 April 1961. The data are now being analysed and the first county report, relating to London, was published in March 1963. Further county reports, and additional specialized reports, have since been published and are still appearing. It will be some time yet before a comprehensive analysis of the whole Census of England and Wales can be prepared and attention is therefore being directed in this study to the London area only.

Immigrants are defined as people born outside the United Kingdom, and we shall ignore the question of nationality or citizenship. It follows that the son of London-born parents, who was himself born outside England, must be regarded as immigrant, whilst the child of Jamaican parents born in England is not an immigrant. Thus no rigid relationship can be inferred between place of birth and racial characteristics or nationality, although it is reasonable to assume that marginal cases are at present few, except in the very young age groups. This will not necessarily be true in the 1971 and subsequent Censuses—the coloured children now being born in Britain, for instance, in most cases possess dual nationality.

Two general points must be made before we examine the Census statistics. The information obtained from the general public is not completely accurate, as the Census authorities themselves testify—questions are sometimes misunderstood, for example. But there is a further difficulty when one considers immigrants, and especially coloured immigrants. Many of the latter are living in overcrowded conditions and have no desire to advertise their presence, particularly to officials of local government housing departments. The secrecy of the Census forms and the distinction between one set of government officials and another are not clearly understood by many recent arrivals, particularly coloured people who do not speak English.

The accuracy of the Census return, in such cases, depended to no small extent upon the zeal of the enumerator who had to collect the schedule, and this was probably not uniform throughout the country. There is, therefore, a strong possibility that under-counting of some immigrant groups was much more serious than amongst the population at large, and we must accept the possibility that the information given on the Census schedules is of different degrees of reliability.

A second point concerns the geographical area under discussion. There are many 'Londons', defined differently for different purposes, but our present concern (following the Census report which in turn follows local government boundaries existing at the time of the Census) is with the London of the administrative county comprising, at its heart, the ancient City of London surrounded by twenty-eight metropolitan boroughs.

Before turning to a study of the immigrant population as such we should glance briefly at the London population as a whole. The following two paragraphs are taken from the official commentary on population change in London and set the background to a study of specific immigrant groups.

The population of London at the 1961 Census of population was 3,200,484. Of this total 4,767 were enumerated in the City of London and the remainder in the twenty-eight Metropolitan boroughs which ranged in population from Wandsworth (347,442 population), Islington (228,345), Lambeth (223,763) and Lewisham (221,753) to Finsbury (32,887) and Holborn (22,008).

Between 1951 and 1961 the population of London fell by 147,472 which represented a rate of 0·45 per cent per year. This rate of decrease was about a third of the average between 1931 and 1951 which indicates some slowing up of the fall in population. The balance of births and deaths between the census dates would have produced a natural increase of 0·46 per cent per year which implies a loss by migration at a rate of 0·90 per cent per year.[1]

In view of the widespread concern at the drift of population to 'London' it at first seems surprising that the population of 'London' is contracting. The fact is, of course, that as in most British cities, the population of London is tending to move into the surrounding counties. Indeed native Londoners are moving out to a somewhat greater extent than the official figures at

[1] *Census 1961: England and Wales—County Report*, London, H.M.S.O., p. xv.

TABLE 5

*Birthplaces of London Residents, April 1961*

| Where born | Number of residents in London | Per cent of residents |
|---|---|---|
| England | 2,553,609 | 80 |
| Scotland | 59,704 | 2 |
| Wales | 48,437 | 2 |
| N. Ireland | 21,202 | 1 |
| Channel Islands, Isle of Man | 2,436 | |
| Born in U.K., birthplace stated | 2,685,388 | 85 |
| Born in U.K., birthplace not stated | 10,619 | |
| Total born in U.K. | 2,696,007 | 85 |
| Irish Republic | 131,703 | 4 |
| Ireland (part not stated) | 9,236 | |
| British Isles | 2,836,946 | 89 |
| Outside British Isles | 321,031 | 10 |
| Birthplace not stated | 16,691 | 1 |
| Total London residents | 3,174,668 | 100 |
| Visitors | 25,816 | |
| All enumerated in London | 3,200,484 | |

*Source:* Census 1961, London County Report

(Of those born outside the British Isles 56% came from a Commonwealth country.)

first glance suggest. As the native Londoners move out the immigrant groups move in, particularly into certain clearly defined areas of the metropolis. In 1951 out of every 1,000 residents in London (from now on reference to 'London' is exclusively to the County of London as covered by the Census report), 93 could be classified as 'immigrants', in the sense that they were born outside England, Wales, Scotland or Northern Ireland. In 1961 this figure had risen to 141—an increase of 52%. To put it another way—whilst the total resident population declined by 4% the 'immigrant' population proportion rose by 44%.

In April 1961, 80% of the residents of London had been born in England, 2% in Scotland, 2% in Wales and 1% in Northern Ireland. Of the remaining 15% born outside the United Kingdom the largest single group came from Eire, and consisted of

4% of the total population. Thus 10% were born outside the British Isles whilst 1% did not state their birthplaces (Table 5). Not all the boroughs of London have had the same experience regarding changes in their immigrant populations in the last few years or in the proportion of immigrants recorded in their populations. The borough with the highest number of recorded immigrants in 1961 was Paddington, with over a quarter of the population being so classified. Woolwich, Southwark, Shoreditch, Poplar, Lewisham, Greenwich, Deptford, Camberwell, Bethnal Green and Bermondsey had less than one immigrant

TABLE 6

*Distribution of Immigrants in London, 1951 and 1961*
*(Borough Analysis)*

| | Resident immigrants per 1,000 of total population | | |
| | | | Increase |
| Borough | In 1951 | In 1961 | 1951–61 |
|---|---|---|---|
| Paddington | 208 | 294 | 86 |
| Kensington | 226 | 289 | 63 |
| Hampstead | 251 | 286 | 35 |
| St. Marylebone | 200 | 220 | 20 |
| Westminster | 187 | 203 | 16 |
| St. Pancras | 133 | 200 | 67 |
| Islington | 72 | 189 | 117 |
| Holborn | 174 | 197 | 23 |
| Stoke Newington | 105 | 192 | 87 |
| Hammersmith | 101 | 190 | 89 |
| Chelsea | 164 | 187 | 23 |
| Hackney | 88 | 142 | 54 |
| Lambeth | 70 | 138 | 68 |
| Fulham | 82 | 137 | 55 |
| Stepney | 123 | 136 | 13 |
| Wandsworth | 74 | 108 | 34 |
| Finsbury | 66 | 108 | 42 |
| Battersea | 46 | 101 | 55 |
| Camberwell | 42 | 84 | 42 |
| Deptford | 33 | 79 | 46 |
| Southwark | 49 | 75 | 26 |
| Bermondsey | 28 | 73 | 45 |
| Bethnal Green | 49 | 66 | 17 |
| Poplar | 34 | 61 | 27 |
| Lewisham | 34 | 58 | 24 |
| Shoreditch | 36 | 50 | 14 |
| Greenwich | 41 | 49 | 8 |
| Woolwich | 41 | 44 | 3 |

*Source:* Census 1961, London County Report

to every ten of the total population. The boroughs also varied regarding changes in the proportion of immigrants in their populations since 1951 (the date of the previous Census). Hammersmith, Islington, Paddington and Stoke Newington showed a substantial increase whereas Woolwich, Westminster, Stepney, Shoreditch, Greenwich and Bethnal Green showed an increase much lower than that of London as a whole. The experience of all the twenty-eight metropolitan boroughs in this regard is summarized above where they are arranged in descending order of the proportion of immigrants within their populations in 1961 (Table 6).

No attempt has so far been made to distinguish between different groups of immigrants, and no specific reference has been made to coloured people, but there are certain boroughs— and parts of boroughs—in London which are now of distinctly mixed racial composition, although even in Paddington the most densely populated 'coloured' area in London, the number of coloured people is considerably less than one in ten of the total population of the borough. In certain parts of most boroughs the density is known to be higher than for the borough as a whole, but this cannot be demonstrated from the published Census tables. The extent to which it is misleading simply to take the average figure for the borough as a whole is brought out clearly in the cases of Lambeth and Kensington. In both of them the average density of the coloured population is between 55 and 65 per thousand, but in each case the coloured people are largely concentrated in the north of the borough. Thus the density of coloured people in the areas of coloured settlement in each borough is very much higher than in the borough as a whole.

In April 1961, there were 321,031 residents of London—10% of the total recorded population—who stated that their birthplace was outside the British Isles, but of these people nearly three-quarters came from only fourteen countries (if the Caribbean area—excluding Jamaica—is regarded for this purpose as one country). The Commonwealth had provided in 1961 just over half of the immigrant population—with Jamaica, from which island came 12% of the immigrants, in the lead. The Caribbean area (excluding Jamaica), Cyprus and India were also of noticeable significance. Outside the Commonwealth Poland was the largest single supplier of immigrants, with Italy and Germany a little behind.[1] In the following table countries which provided more than 5,000 immigrants for the resident population of London are separately listed.

TABLE 7

*Residents of London in April 1961, whose Stated Birthplaces were outside the British Isles*

| Birthplace | Number of persons | Per cent of persons born outside U.K. |
|---|---|---|
| *Commonwealth* | | |
| Jamaica | 37,061 | 12 |
| Caribbean* | 33,427 | 10 |
| Cyprus | 26,308 | 8 |
| India | 24,592 | 8 |
| Australia | 8,367 | 3 |
| Nigeria | 6,160 | 2 |
| Others | 42,455 | 13 |
| TOTAL Commonwealth | 178,370 | 56 |
| *Non-Commonwealth and at sea* | | |
| Poland | 22,473 | 7 |
| Italy | 17,760 | 6 |
| Germany | 17,379 | 5 |
| U.S.S.R. | 10,124 | 3 |
| Union of S. Africa | 7,798 | 2 |
| Austria | 7,640 | 2 |
| France | 7,417 | 2 |
| Spain | 7,293 | 2 |
| Others | 44,777 | 15 |
| TOTAL Non-Commonwealth | 142,661 | 44 |

*Source:* Census 1961, London County Report

\* British Commonwealth territories in the Caribbean area, excluding Jamaica.

It is possible to obtain from the published Census tables an analysis of the age structure of the total population of London, but not for the separate immigrant groups within that population. This is obtainable from the seven-borough analysis. We can examine the seven boroughs as one group since there is no important variation between them, as the Jamaican households (to use one example) show.[2] In only one case is the devia-

[1] It will be observed that Ireland, although outside the United Kingdom, is within the British Isles and therefore excluded altogether from these statistics.

[2] 'Jamaican households' are defined as groups of persons recorded as living at one address where the first person listed on the Census schedule was born in Jamaica. A similar terminology will be applied to 'Polish households', etc., to avoid the circumlocution involved in the phrase 'households where the first person on the list was born in . . .'.

tion of a borough from the average as high as 6%—in most other cases the deviation is less than 5%. It is probably safe to assume that—with the possible exception of Paddington—the deviations are due to random forces and do not reflect any statistically significant differences in the borough populations. This analysis of each borough separately for each separate immigrant group to check that the deviation does not exceed 5% from the average has been systematically carried out throughout this investigation. There is no point in recording the experience of each borough separately *unless* the figures reveal a significant difference between them, which they do not, and henceforth we shall concern ourselves, so far as the age groups are concerned, with average figures drawn from an aggregation of the seven separate boroughs (Table 8).

TABLE 8

*Age Groups of Persons living in Jamaican Households in Seven London Boroughs (1961)*

| | Men | (per cent) | Women | |
|---|---|---|---|---|
| *Borough* | *Under 30* | *Under 50* | *Under 30* | *Under 5c* |
| Lambeth | 55 | 96 | 60 | 97 |
| Stoke Newington | 56 | 97 | 64 | 97 |
| Hackney | 55 | 96 | 62 | 97 |
| Paddington | 50 | 95 | 55 | 95 |
| Deptford | 55 | 97 | 63 | 97 |
| Battersea | 51 | 96 | 60 | 96 |
| Camberwell | 55 | 96 | 63 | 98 |
| Average | 54 | 96 | 61 | 97 |
| Number of persons | 13,080 | | 11,907 | |

*Source:* full Census analysis

We can, if we wish, from the published Census tables break this analysis down further by considering each borough separately, but what we *cannot* do is to distinguish between the various racial and ethnic groups within the total population. In order to do this we must rely on the sample of seven London boroughs and derive information which relates to the seven selected immigrant categories and the households with a person born in England at the head. As Table 9 shows, the age structure of the London population generally is very similar to the 'English' households in our sample of seven boroughs.

## TABLE 9

### Age Structure of Selected Household Groups in the London Population, 1961

#### (a) MALES
*Seven boroughs only*

| Age group | Total population of London: all boroughs and City of London | Households with head born in (per cent) | | | | | | | |
|---|---|---|---|---|---|---|---|---|---|
| | | England | Jamaica | Caribbean | India | Pakistan | Poland | Cyprus | Ireland |
| 0–4 | 7 | 7 | 17 | 16 | 10 | 9 | 6 | 16 | 15 |
| 5–9 | 6 | 6 | 4 | 4 | 7 | 5 | 6 | 10 | 10 |
| 10–14 | 7 | 8 | 3 | 2 | 6 | 5 | 6 | 7 | 7 |
| 15–19 | 7 | 7 | 4 | 4 | 7 | 4 | 4 | 8 | 6 |
| 20–24 | 8 | 7 | 11 | 15 | 11 | 12 | 5 | 13 | 10 |
| 25–29 | 8 | 7 | 16 | 20 | 15 | 25 | 4 | 13 | 10 |
| TOTAL under 30 | 44 | 42 | 54 | 61 | 55 | 60 | 31 | 67 | 57 |
| 30–34 | 7 | 7 | 16 | 16 | 12 | 15 | 6 | 10 | 9 |
| 35–39 | 7 | 7 | 12 | 10 | 9 | 9 | 10 | 7 | 8 |
| 40–44 | 7 | 7 | 8 | 6 | 5 | 6 | 7 | 5 | 7 |
| 45–49 | 7 | 8 | 5 | 4 | 4 | 4 | 9 | 3 | 7 |
| 50–54 | 7 | 8 | 2 | 2 | 4 | 1 | 8 | 3 | 5 |
| 55–59 | 6 | 7 | 1 | 1 | 4 | 3 | 8 | 1 | 3 |
| TOTAL under 60 | 43 | 44 | 44 | 39 | 38 | 38 | 48 | 30 | 39 |
| 60 and over | 14 | 15 | 1 | 1 | 6 | 2 | 21 | 3 | 4 |
| Number of persons | 1,524,359 | 12,438† | 13,080 | 7,976 | 3,248 | 478 | 5,183 | 4,194 | 22,410 |

## TABLE 9 (*cont.*)

### (b) FEMALES
#### Seven boroughs only

| Age group | Total population of London: all boroughs and City of London | Households with head born in (per cent) | | | | | | | |
|---|---|---|---|---|---|---|---|---|---|
| | | England | Jamaica | Caribbean | India | Pakistan | Poland | Cyprus | Ireland |
| 0–4 | 7 | 6 | 19 | 19 | 11 | 15 | 6 | 16 | 14 |
| 5–9 | 5 | 6 | 5 | 5 | 8 | 10 | 7 | 10 | 9 |
| 10–14 | 6 | 7 | 3 | 3 | 7 | 7 | 5 | 8 | 7 |
| 15–19 | 7 | 6 | 5 | 6 | 6 | 7 | 4 | 9 | 6 |
| 20–24 | 8 | 7 | 12 | 17 | 11 | 15 | 4 | 14 | 10 |
| 25–29 | 7 | 5 | 17 | 19 | 10 | 14 | 5 | 13 | 10 |
| TOTAL under 30 | 40 | 37 | 61 | 70 | 53 | 68 | 30 | 70 | 58 |
| 30–34 | 6 | 6 | 15 | 13 | 8 | 11 | 8 | 9 | 9 |
| 35–39 | 7 | 7 | 10 | 7 | 7 | 7 | 8 | 6 | 8 |
| 40–44 | 6 | 6 | 7 | 4 | 6 | 2 | 5 | 4 | 6 |
| 45–49 | 7 | 7 | 4 | 3 | 5 | 4 | 7 | 4 | 6 |
| 50–54 | 7 | 7 | 2 | 1 | 5 | 2 | 9 | 3 | 4 |
| 55–59 | 6 | 7 | 1 | 1 | 4 | 2 | 8 | 2 | 3 |
| TOTAL under 60 | 40 | 40 | 39 | 29 | 35 | 28 | 45 | 28 | 36 |
| 60 and over | 20 | 22 | —* | 1 | 11 | 4 | 25 | 2 | 7 |
| Number of persons | 1,676,125 | 13,850† | 11,907 | 6,873 | 2,882 | 262 | 4,953 | 3,819 | 21,858 |

* Under 0·5%.   † 1 in 25 sample.

*Source:* Census 1961, London County Report and full Census analysis

The striking fact which emerges is the very high proportion of children recorded amongst West Indians (Jamaicans and Caribbeans). One person in five in West Indian households in these seven London boroughs was under the age of nine years, and the great majority of them were under five. This high proportion of young children (many of whom were undoubtedly born in England) contrasts with the very low level in the immediately higher age groups which probably results from the fact that so many of the West Indian migrants have left their children behind.[1]

Since the Census was taken West Indians have continued to enter Britain and in the first year of the operation of the Act, up to June 1963, 24% of the admissions from the West Indies (but only 15% of the departures) were children under fifteen years of age. In the second year of the operation of the Act almost one-third of the *net inflow* from the West Indies consisted of children. The imbalance shown by the Census tables in the household structure of West Indians is therefore being adjusted by immigration, but since well over 90% of the children of West Indian migrants were left in the West Indies when their parents migrated to Britain it will be a long time, if ever, before West Indians show the same balanced age structure as the English households.

Among Cypriot, Caribbean and Pakistani households the number of younger persons under thirty years of age was very high—between 60 and 70% compared with 40% among English households. The Jamaicans, Indians and Irish recorded a lower proportion of between 50 and 60% under thirty years of age. The Polish households show a noticeable divergence from all the other groups. In their case only 30% of the individuals were under the age of thirty, whilst 24% (as compared with less than 5% in the case of Jamaicans, Caribbeans, Pakistani and Cypriot) were sixty years of age or over. The age structure of the Polish households may be due to the fact that few children were born during the second World War and that a considerable number of ex-servicemen in the age group of twenty to forty years migrated to other Commonwealth countries and the Americas just after the War.

These figures indicate clearly the extent to which the social needs of the various immigrant groups differ from those of the

[1] See Davison, *West Indian Migrants*.

population of London as a whole. Day nurseries and Primary schools are at present of relatively greater importance to Jamaican households than are old-age pensions. Polish households, on the other hand, are likely to be much more interested in the development of social services for the elderly and infirm and the retirement age, matters which hardly concern the West Indians, Pakistanis, Cypriots and Irish in England at present (Table 10).

## TABLE 10

### Ages of Immigrant Groups under 21 Years of Age
### Both sexes (per cent, totalling 100)

| Years | | Eng. | Jam. | Car. | Ind. | Pak. | Pol. | Iri. | Cyp. |
|---|---|---|---|---|---|---|---|---|---|
| 0 under | 1 | 5·0 | 14·5 | 16·2 | 7·7 | 8·8 | 4·6 | 8·4 | 8·3 |
| 1 ,, | 2 | 5·8 | 13·2 | 13·3 | 6·7 | 7·4 | 4·4 | 8·2 | 7·7 |
| 2 ,, | 3 | 4·4 | 12·0 | 11·9 | 6·8 | 8·3 | 6·3 | 7·1 | 6·6 |
| 3 ,, | 4 | 4·3 | 9·9 | 8·4 | 5·9 | 6·6 | 5·2 | 6·7 | 6·6 |
| 4 ,, | 5 | 4·2 | 7·5 | 5·1 | 4·7 | 4·8 | 5·8 | 6·5 | 6·6 |
| 5 ,, | 6 | 4·2 | 4·9 | 3·4 | 5·3 | 7·9 | 5·3 | 5·9 | 6·1 |
| 6 ,, | 7 | 3·8 | 2·7 | 2·3 | 4·3 | 3·0 | 5·5 | 5·1 | 5·0 |
| 7 ,, | 8 | 4·3 | 2·4 | 2·4 | 3·8 | 5·2 | 5·7 | 4·7 | 4·0 |
| 8 ,, | 9 | 4·2 | 2·0 | 2·0 | 4·1 | 3·0 | 5·8 | 4·4 | 4·0 |
| 9 ,, | 10 | 4·2 | 2·1 | 2·4 | 4·3 | 2·2 | 6·0 | 4·3 | 3·9 |
| 10 ,, | 11 | 4·3 | 2·2 | 2·0 | 3·8 | 3·5 | 5·7 | 4·0 | 3·1 |
| 11 ,, | 12 | 4·2 | 2·0 | 1·7 | 3·6 | 3·9 | 5·0 | 3·6 | 3·5 |
| 12 ,, | 13 | 5·1 | 1·7 | 1·6 | 3·1 | 3·0 | 5·4 | 3·4 | 3·7 |
| 13 ,, | 14 | 5·9 | 1·8 | 1·6 | 4·0 | 5·2 | 3·3 | 3·5 | 3·3 |
| 14 ,, | 15 | 6·6 | 1·6 | 1·7 | 4·8 | 2·2 | 4·0 | 3·1 | 2·9 |
| 15 ,, | 16 | 4·7 | 1·3 | 1·9 | 3·7 | 3·9 | 3·0 | 2·6 | 3·1 |
| 16 ,, | 17 | 5·0 | 1·8 | 2·0 | 4·2 | 3·0 | 4·1 | 2·8 | 2·8 |
| 17 ,, | 18 | 4·2 | 2·6 | 2·9 | 4·0 | 2·2 | 2·9 | 2·8 | 4·0 |
| 18 ,, | 19 | 5·4 | 3·4 | 3·7 | 4·1 | 3·5 | 3·5 | 3·6 | 3·5 |
| 19 ,, | 20 | 4·7 | 4·4 | 5·4 | 4·5 | 4·4 | 3·0 | 4·1 | 4·7 |
| 20 ,, | 21 | 4·8 | 5·0 | 7·1 | 5·3 | 7·0 | 4·4 | 4·4 | 5·3 |
| Number | | 7,359 | 7,735 | 4,691 | 1,986 | 227 | 2,260 | 17,103 | 3,539 |

Source: full Census analysis

## Marital Status

A private household was defined during the Census enumeration in the following terms:

A household comprises one person living alone or a group of persons living together, partaking of meals prepared together and benefiting from a common housekeeping. A person or persons living, but not boarding with a household in a house, flat, etc., should be treated as a separate household. But a person living with a household who usually has at least one main meal a day provided by that household while in residence is part of that household. (Breakfast counts as a meal for this purpose.) A household must have exclusive use of at least one room. If two people share one room and do not have exclusive use of at least one other room they should be treated as one household. [1]

We must remember that the reliability of replies to the Census questionnaire undoubtedly varies between immigrant groups and it differs according to the type of question which is asked. It may well be that questions about marital status are not likely to be answered with a high degree of truthfulness; different social customs in the home country may affect the position. An unmarried couple living together as man and wife in England may not have disclosed to each other that they are already married and would therefore be most unlikely to reply truthfully on a Census questionnaire. On the other hand, such a couple may claim to be married to each other when, in law, this is not the case. These problems arise over census-taking in every country and there is no practical way of checking the quality of the replies. We have no alternative but to take the replies as given on the Census form as the nearest approximation to the truth we can reach and study the figures with this limitation in mind.

The raw data produced by the computer provided an age and sex breakdown for eight separate groups of household, classified by the birthplace of the head of the household, for each of the seven selected boroughs separately, showing the numbers of persons who were single, married, widowed or divorced in each case. There were thus 8,960 separate categories to be considered and some condensation of the data, in order to make it manageable, is unavoidable. The seven boroughs did not individually deviate markedly from their aggregate experience, and Table 11 gives a composite picture.

Table 11 shows, as might be expected, that (apart from Polish immigrants) all other immigrant groups tend to consist of fewer married people than does the 'English' population. Of course, the figures depend on the meaning given by people to 'marriage', and in this connection the rather special social traditions of the West Indies need to be considered.

[1] The present enquiry is confined solely to private households—persons living in public institutions are excluded from the statistics.

## TABLE II

### Marital Status of Selected Household Groups

| | MALES | | | | FEMALES | | | |
| --- | --- | --- | --- | --- | --- | --- | --- | --- |
| | Number of persons | Per cent | | | Number of persons | Per cent | | |
| | | Single | Married | Widowed or divorced | | Single | Married | Widowed or divorced |
| Whole London population | 1,524,359 | 46 | 51 | 3 | 1,676,125 | 41 | 46 | 13 |
| Households in which the head was born in: | | | | | | | | |
| | *Seven boroughs* | | | | | | | |
| England* | 12,438 | 42 | 54 | 4 | 13,850 | 37 | 49 | 13 |
| Jamaica | 13,080 | 56 | 44 | — | 11,907 | 55 | 44 | 1 |
| Caribbean | 7,976 | 59 | 40 | 1 | 6,873 | 56 | 42 | 2 |
| India | 3,248 | 56 | 42 | 2 | 2,882 | 46 | 43 | 10 |
| Pakistan | 478 | 55 | 42 | 2 | 262 | 51 | 44 | 5 |
| Poland | 5,183 | 43 | 52 | 5 | 4,953 | 32 | 52 | 16 |
| Ireland | 22,410 | 55 | 43 | 1 | 21,858 | 50 | 45 | 4 |
| Cyprus | 4,194 | 54 | 45 | 1 | 3,819 | 48 | 48 | 5 |

Source: Census 1961, London County Report and full Census analysis

* 1 in 25 sample.

In the study of the random sample prior to their departure from Jamaica it was found[1] that about 22 % of the persons interviewed claimed to be legally married. This compared with 24 % from the island of Dominica where completely separate data were obtained from official records. It will be seen from Table 12 that the proportion claiming to be legally married increased sharply in the first year to 45 % of the total and then again in the second year to 52 %. Efforts were made in the second year to find out how many of those legally married were in fact living with their marital partners. There can be no doubt that the majority of Jamaicans very quickly change their attitude towards marriage when they migrate to England and couples who would have lived together indefinitely in Jamaica without marrying legalize their relationship quite quickly after their arrival in Britain.

TABLE 12

*Marital Status of Jamaicans (per cent)*

| Marital status | In Jamaica | End of first year in England | End of second year in England |
|---|---|---|---|
| Legally married | 22* | 45 | 52† |
| Not legally married | 78 | 55 | 48 |
| *Of those not legally married* | | 100 | |
| Living with an unmarried consort | | | 30 |
| Alone or with relatives | | | 70 |
| | | | 100 |

*Source:* Jamaican Sample Survey

\* In the West Indian island of Dominica, official records have shown that 24% of the migrants from that island were legally married. See Table 11 in *West Indian Migrants*.

† Of those legally married 84% were recorded as living with their spouses, and 16% living separately at the end of the second year.

It often comes as something of a shock to English people on their first arrival in the West Indies to discover that the majority of the children born there are illegitimate. According to statistics recently published which were derived from the 1960

[1] *West Indian Migrants*, Table 12, p. 18.

Census of Population in Jamaica,[1] 43% of the total female population of that island were classified as single, 29% were married, 19% were living in what are called 'common law unions' (that is to say living in a relatively stable cohabitation without legal recognition of the union), whilst a further 9% were widowed, divorced or did not state their marital condition. Seven out of every ten females above the age of fifteen had borne at least one child in 1960. Of the total female population above the age of fifteen only about one in three (32%) were actually living with a legal husband, 21% had never lived with a partner, 22% were living with a 'common law' partner, 24% had lived at some time with a common law partner but were no longer doing so at the time of the Census. The explanation for this state of affairs must be sought primarily in the historical evolution of the society: in the days of slavery, marriage was severely discouraged, if not forbidden, amongst slaves by plantation-owners who themselves not infrequently set an example which was hardly likely to elevate the conception of Christian marriage in the minds of African people who had come in the first place from largely polygamous societies. Despite the efforts of the Christian churches to change the situation, marriage as a social institution is regarded as an unattainable ideal by many of the women in Jamaica today and little or no social stigma (although considerable economic difficulty) is experienced by the unmarried young girl who becomes pregnant in her later teens. More often than not the baby is left in the care of the grandmother whilst the girl endeavours to find employment to support herself and her child. One of the reasons why men in Jamaica are reluctant to undertake the responsibilities of marriage is the high degree of unemployment in the island, and the general job insecurity which so many of them experience. This state of mind cannot simply be dismissed by the mere fact of crossing the Atlantic and coming to live in Britain, although in the very different economic and social climate of Britain the West Indian migrants find themselves subject to forces which increase their willingness to marry and take on the responsibility of establishing a settled home and family. Quite apart from the increased economic security which many of the women have once they have found

[1] O. C. Francis, *The People of Modern Jamaica*, Jamaica, Department of Statistics (Census Officer).

their feet in Britain, many social institutions (for instance the income tax laws) and the prospect of steady employment make marriage a much more attractive proposition for the males.

Often the married couple live as part of a complicated network of relatives, and not infrequently the children in the household are the offspring of one of the partners only who has previously consorted with someone else. It is not unusual to find a husband and wife each with a child from another partner living with them and one or more children from their own union as well. One family visited during the sample survey consisted of a husband and wife living in one room but eating with sister-in-law, sister-in-law's husband and baby, all living in another street. The wife often cooks for more than one man: in the case, for instance, where the husband and wife rented the house from an uncle with three other Jamaican men as lodgers, the wife cooked and cleaned for all five. It was not unusual to find people—particularly those living alone—living in one house but eating in another. A typical case was Mr. P. (as we may call him), who lived separately in that he paid rent to his brother for one room and cooked his own food, but in other respects was an integral part of the brother's family.

As the proportion of legally married has risen, the proportion recorded as living in a more or less stable relationship with an unmarried consort declined from 22% during the original enquiry in Jamaica to 16% at the end of the second year in Britain, by which time only one-third of the sample were recorded as living alone or with blood relatives such as brothers, cousins, aunts or parents. In many of the cases where unmarried couples were living together, there were clear indications that they intended to get married in due course. Often the advent of a baby provides the necessary catalyst for action. The attitude of the males, particularly, in such cases is well illustrated by Mr. D., who said that he intended to marry as soon as he and his mate had settled in Britain, but that it was just one of those things he had not yet done. It must be remembered that a wedding in Jamaica is likely to be an elaborate, and therefore an expensive affair. It is an occasion for conspicuous consumption on the grand scale and is often regarded as the culmination of some years of successful cohabitation rather than the initial ceremony. Jamaicans in Britain can afford to get married (there are also perhaps fewer relatives to entertain at the wedding) and the whole ethos of the society impels them towards marriage. They react to their new environment in the main by tending to conform to it. There is little reason to doubt that the trend will continue.

## Size of Households

We can derive some information regarding the household structure of the various immigrant households from the Census analysis. We would, ideally, like to know the number of adults and children living in the various households in the different immigrant groups but it was not possible during the present enquiry to pursue this question from the Census data, although the sample survey amongst Jamaicans casts a certain amount of light on this subject as far as the Jamaican immigrants are concerned. We know, from the Census analysis, the total number of households which had a person born in one of the eight selected countries as its head, and we know the number of persons recorded as living in those households. Taking all the seven boroughs together, analysed separately for the eight selected household groups, we arrive at the position recorded in Table 13. (As before, the figures for each borough were calculated

TABLE 13

### Numbers living in Households (Seven London Boroughs)

| Birthplace of head of household | Number of households | Number of persons living in those households | Average number of persons per household |
|---|---|---|---|
| Cyprus | 1,891 | 8,013 | 4·23 |
| Jamaica | 7,597 | 24,987 | 3·28 |
| Ireland | 13,914 | 44,268 | 3·18 |
| Caribbean | 5,211 | 14,849 | 2·84 |
| India | 2,190 | 6,130 | 2·79 |
| Pakistan | 269 | 740 | 2·75 |
| England | 9,604* | 26,288* | 2·74 |
| Poland | 3,793 | 10,136 | 2·67 |

Source: full Census analysis

* 1 in 25 sample.

separately during the course of the analysis and there is no significant difference between them.) The table is arranged in descending order of household size and calls for little comment.

The largest households are those headed by a person born in Cyprus, followed by the Jamaicans, then the Irish. Households headed by persons born in England and Poland, it will be observed, are at the foot of the list with households of about two-thirds the size of those headed by persons born in Cyprus.

To supplement the information obtained from the Census, the structure of the Jamaican households covered by the Jamaican survey was analysed in a little more detail to show the number of adults and children living in the group as a whole. The information thus collected is summarized below in the form of a matrix in Table 14 which gives the proportion of the households in the sample with a given number of adults and children.

TABLE 14

*Structure of Jamaican Households (per cent)*

| Adults | None | One | Children (under 16) Two | Three or more |
|---|---|---|---|---|
| One | 36 | 2 | — | — |
| Two | 32 | 7 | 2 | * |
| Three | 3 | 4 | 1 | — |
| Four or more | 5 | 3 | 3 | 3 |

Source: Jamaican Sample Survey

* Less than 0·5%.

Just over a third of the 'households' thus enumerated consisted of one person living alone. A further third consisted of a couple living together without children. It must be remembered that these figures relate to the household in England: many of the people classified as living alone in England, or with a partner and no children, may well have a partner (or a different partner) in Jamaica and a high proportion of them have children who have been left behind in Jamaica.[1]

At the 1961 Census, persons aged fifteen and over, living in one household in every ten, were asked to state the age at which they terminated their education.[2] Because this enquiry related

---

[1] *West Indian Migrants*, Table 31, p. 70.

[2] This question did not apply to persons who were still receiving full-time education at school, college, university, etc. For persons who were not receiving full-time education, but intending to resume it later, the respondents were asked to state the age at which education was discontinued. For students actually enrolled in a course of full-time study which involved spending part of the time in employment, no information was required.

to only 10% of the London population, it was decided to secure information in the present enquiry relating to the seven selected groups of immigrant households, and those where the head was born in England, on a one-in-twenty-five sample basis, for all the twenty-eight metropolitan boroughs in the County of London. The information resulting from this enquiry, showing the position in the twenty-eight boroughs, is summarized in Table 15.

## TABLE 15

### Terminal Education Age, 1961

|  | (a) MALES Per cent | | | | | | | |
|  |  |  | Persons born in | | | | | |
| Age at which education terminated | Eng.* | Jam. | Car. | Ind. | Pak. | Pol. | Ire. | Cyp. |
| 15 years and under | 80 | 76 | 63 | 24 | 34 | 48 | 76 | 84 |
| 16–19 | 17 | 22 | 33 | 44 | 37 | 21 | 20 | 13 |
| 20 and over | 4 | 2 | 4 | 31 | 29 | 30 | 3 | 2 |
| TOTAL | 100 | 100 | 100 | 100 | 100 | 100 | 100 | 100 |
| Number where terminal age stated | 3,306 | 1,181 | 1,089 | 949 | 179 | 1,069 | 5,431 | 737 |
| Still students | 109 | 20 | 65 | 152 | 22 | 12 | 32 | 49 |
| Not stated | 286 | 274 | 214 | 193 | 43 | 220 | 845 | 182 |
|  | (b) FEMALES Per cent | | | | | | | |
| 15 years and under | 79 | 69 | 61 | 28 | 25 | 50 | 69 | 88 |
| 16–19 | 18 | 27 | 35 | 60 | 50 | 32 | 29 | 10 |
| 20 and over | 2 | 3 | 4 | 12 | 25 | 18 | 2 | 1 |
| TOTAL | 100 | 100 | 100 | 100 | 100 | 100 | 100 | 100 |
| Number where terminal age stated | 3,881 | 1,050 | 846 | 871 | 60 | 666 | 6,099 | 565 |
| Still students | 103 | 20 | 36 | 54 | 3 | 8 | 45 | 24 |
| Not stated | 351 | 238 | 168 | 107 | 5 | 186 | 945 | 164 |

*Source:* 10% Census analysis

* 1 in 25 sample.

This table is based upon an analysis of replies relating to 27,979 individuals, half of whom were males and half females. Of this total 2% said they were still students, 13% did not reply to the question at all, and 85% gave a definite age at which they said they had terminated their full-time education. The proportion recorded as still receiving full-time education varied considerably between the different immigrant groups (see Table 16). In most cases the proportion of male students was equal to, or usually greater than, the proportion of female students except in the case of Jamaicans. In this case, the female proportion was slightly in excess of the male, possibly because of the number of girls training to be nurses who may have been included, perhaps erroneously, as full-time students. In the case of both males and females the proportion of Indian and Pakistani students exceeded the other groups by a noticeable margin, whereas in the case of the Irish and the Polish individuals the student proportion was much lower than the average. As we have seen, the Polish individuals have a much larger proportion of their number in the older age groups.

TABLE 16

*Proportion of Persons who had not completed*
*Full-Time Education (per cent)*

| Persons born in | Males | Females |
|---|---|---|
| England | 2·9 | 2·3 |
| Jamaica | 1·3 | 1·5 |
| Caribbean | 4·7 | 3·4 |
| India | 11·7 | 5·2 |
| Pakistan | 9·0 | 4·4 |
| Poland | 0·9 | 0·9 |
| Ireland | 0·5 | 0·6 |
| Cyprus | 5·0 | 3·1 |

*Source:* 10% Census analysis

The obvious question that arises is whether these statistics of age of terminal education are accurate. Is it likely, for example, that such a high proportion of both men and women from India and Pakistan would have continued at school after the age of fifteen? It is not easy to put any clear interpretation upon the statistics which have resulted from this part of the Census enquiry, and it is important not to assume that there is necessarily a positive correlation between the age at which full-time education was stated to have terminated and the level of educational attainment achieved. We see from Table 15 that 80% of the males born in England (79% of the females) said they had terminated their education before their sixteenth year, whilst 21% of the males (20% of the females) continued to some form of higher education. In the English context this seems to be a reasonable result. The same cannot be said for the results obtained relating to persons born in India. Here, taken at their face value, the statistics indicate that 75 % of the males and 72 % of the females continued their full-time education after the age of fifteen. We cannot, from the Census returns themselves, offer any explanation for this large difference, but three points should be borne in mind in this connection. The respondents may have misunderstood the question on the Census form or deliberately stated a false terminal age for prestige reasons. If this is so it does not appear to have operated in the case of Jamaicans, Caribbeans or Cypriots. A second, and much more likely, explanation is that persons in the Commonwealth countries tend to remain at school much longer than children normally do in Britain because of the problem of finding employment once they leave school—and also, of course, because many of them start school at a later age. Furthermore the standards of Primary education, due to large classes, poorly trained staff and ill-equipped buildings, tend to be much lower in the overseas Commonwealth than in Britain, and students must remain at school much longer than they need to in Britain even to approximate, on termination of education, to the educational standards reached by the average child in Britain at the age of fifteen.

# Chapter III

## HOUSING CONDITIONS

THE Census provides useful and important information about housing conditions; figures concerned with overcrowding, the use of facilities (water supply, water closet, etc.), and details of tenure, are all available. Again, our comparison between English and immigrant groups can highlight the situation.

### Definitions

We use the terms which are published in the Census. 'Private households' have already been defined,[1] but how far this precise definition can be applied in the confusing household structures which exist amongst Jamaican households—and possibly the other immigrant households also—is impossible to say with any degree of assurance. No doubt great difficulties were experienced by the Census enumerators but we have no alternative but to accept at their face value the schedules they completed as the most accurate result which it was possible to obtain.

A *room* is defined as follows:

A room is any covered space surrounded by walls, doors, or windows and used by the household for living, eating or sleeping. Rooms available for these purposes but not actually in use, e.g. unfurnished spare bedrooms, are included. . . .

Landings, lobbies, recesses, closets and bathrooms are not counted as rooms: nor are store-rooms, offices, warehouses, shops or any other rooms used for non-domestic purposes.

A kitchen, kitchenette or scullery is counted if meals are regularly eaten there, otherwise it is not.

### Density

The definition of 'room' does not say anything about the size of the room, but a rough guide to the density of population (or overcrowding) can be obtained by examining the number of

[1] See page 27.

## TABLE 17

### Rooms occupied by Households headed by a Person born in Jamaica (per cent of persons)

| Households occupying the following number of rooms | Lambeth | Stoke Newington | Hackney | Paddington | Deptford | Battersea | Camberwell | Average of 7 boroughs |
|---|---|---|---|---|---|---|---|---|
| 1 room | 33 | 21 | 30 | 37 | 26 | 19 | 24 | 29 |
| 2 rooms | 18 | 26 | 26 | 22 | 13 | 20 | 17 | 20 |
| 3 rooms | 15 | 17 | 18 | 22 | 18 | 16 | 14 | 16 |
| TOTAL 1–3 rooms | 66 | 64 | 74 | 81 | 57 | 55 | 55 | 65 |
| 4 rooms | 10 | 10 | 8 | 5 | 11 | 11 | 9 | 9 |
| 5 rooms | 6 | 8 | 4 | 5 | 9 | 7 | 10 | 7 |
| 6 rooms | 9 | 9 | 8 | 6 | 9 | 14 | 17 | 10 |
| 7 or more rooms | 8 | 9 | 5 | 3 | 14 | 12 | 10 | 9 |
|  | 100 | 100 | 100 | 100 | 100 | 100 | 100 | 100 |
| Number of persons | 911 | 1,538 | 4,349 | 2,026 | 1,642 | 2,658 | 3,663 | 24,987 |

*Source:* full Census analysis

(This table shows the proportion of persons living in households headed by a person born in Jamaica (not the proportion of households) in each separate borough which occupied a stated number of rooms.)

## TABLE 18

### Rooms occupied by Selected Household Groups (Seven London Boroughs) (per cent of persons)

| Households occupying the following number of rooms | Households in which the head was born in | | | | | | | |
|---|---|---|---|---|---|---|---|---|
| | England | Jamaica | Caribbean | India | Pakistan | Poland | Ireland | Cyprus |
| 1 room | 2 | 29 | 43 | 16 | 22 | 6 | 11 | 7 |
| 2 rooms | 9 | 20 | 24 | 15 | 15 | 12 | 21 | 17 |
| 3 rooms | 29 | 16 | 15 | 21 | 21 | 23 | 27 | 29 |
| TOTAL 1–3 rooms | 40 | 65 | 83 | 52 | 57 | 41 | 59 | 53 |
| 4 rooms | 27 | 9 | 6 | 18 | 12 | 23 | 20 | 19 |
| 5 rooms | 15 | 7 | 3 | 13 | 7 | 12 | 10 | 10 |
| 6 rooms | 12 | 10 | 4 | 9 | 14 | 10 | 7 | 11 |
| 7 or more rooms | 6 | 9 | 3 | 8 | 10 | 13 | 4 | 6 |
| | 100 | 100 | 100 | 100 | 100 | 100 | 100 | 100 |
| Number of persons | 26,288* | 24,987 | 14,849 | 6,130 | 740 | 10,136 | 44,268 | 8,013 |

Source: full Census analysis

* 1 in 25 sample.

(The above statistics record the proportion of persons living in the households, not the proportion of households.)

persons per room.[1] Table 17 gives the information for Jamaican households in the seven boroughs.

If we consider first the average figures over the seven boroughs taken together we see that almost two persons out of three in these 'Jamaican' households lived in households which occupied three rooms or less, whilst just over one in four (29%) lived in one-room households only. If we examine each borough separately it is clear that there are variations between them. In Paddington four out of five (81%) were living in households which occupied three rooms or less and over one in three (37%) were living in one-room households.

Table 18 shows the picture for all the household groups. It might be argued that the variations between boroughs (Table 17) or between groups (Table 18) might surely be a reflection of the general situation in London; i.e., overcrowding of Jamaicans is high in Paddington because Paddington generally is overcrowded (see Table 17). Or perhaps Caribbeans are overcrowded because they happen to live in generally overcrowded areas (Table 18).

Using as a criterion the number of rooms occupied by households we can see from Table 18 that immigrant groups fare much worse than the English households except in the case of

TABLE 18A

| Household head born in | Per cent of persons in the households living in | |
| | One room | Three rooms or less |
| --- | --- | --- |
| Caribbean | 43 | 83 |
| Jamaica | 29 | 65 |
| Pakistan | 22 | 57 |
| India | 16 | 52 |
| Ireland | 11 | 59 |
| Cyprus | 7 | 53 |
| Poland | 6 | 41 |
| England | 2 | 40 |

households headed by a person born in Poland. People from the Caribbean area (other than Jamaica) with their households

---

[1] If it is the case that the average size of a household in one immigrant group is larger than the average size in another, or if the rooms in one district of London tend to be larger than in another, a straight comparison between rooms occupied by households may give a somewhat misleading impression of degrees of overcrowding. This problem cannot be overcome at present.

appear to be in the least favourable position; then come the Jamaican households. The rank order of the eight household groups is shown on page 41, the least favoured group being at the top of the list.

These statistics of necessity conceal wide variations between the different boroughs. In order to illustrate this point without actually reproducing all the statistics, we may consider the proportion of persons in the different birthplace groups who were living in three rooms or less. In almost every birthplace group (the Indian being the solitary exception) the borough of Paddington records a proportion which is 10% or more above the average for all the seven boroughs. On the other hand, in the borough of Camberwell five out of the eight selected groups recorded a proportion which is 10% or more below the average. The other boroughs vary in their experiences between these two extremes (Table 19).

A study of the number of rooms occupied by households is interesting but is only a limited guide to the degree of over-crowding in one group as compared with another, for it is obvious that the number of rooms required by a household depends on the number of persons living in that household and on the size of the rooms. Table 20 gives an analysis of the various household groups in the seven London boroughs, according to the number of persons per room.

If the number of persons living in a room is taken as a criterion for overcrowding, the situation changes appreciably from that which emerges if we consider the number of rooms occupied by households. We still cannot overcome the problem of different room sizes. Persons living in households headed by a Caribbean are still in the least favourable position and Jamaican households remain in second place. On this different basis Cypriot households have moved into third place and Irish households are in a less advantageous position than Pakistani or Indian. The Polish households are far better off than the newer immigrant groups. Whilst roughly a quarter of the persons living in English and Polish households are living at a density of more than one person per room, three-quarters of the persons living in Caribbean and Jamaican households are doing so. The table brings out clearly the relatively unfavourable position of West Indian households as compared with Indian and Pakistani ones. It also suggests (though it does not

Household Groups occupying three Rooms or less (Seven London Boroughs) (per cent of persons)

| Households in which the head was born in | Lambeth | Stoke Newington | Hackney | Paddington | Depford | Battersea | Camberwell | All seven boroughs Average | All seven boroughs No. of persons |
|---|---|---|---|---|---|---|---|---|---|
| England | 39 | 42 | 41 | 58* | 39 | 39 | 35 | 40 | 10,563† |
| Jamaica | 66 | 64 | 74 | 81* | 57 | 55‡ | 55‡ | 65 | 16,269 |
| Caribbean | 70‡ | 85 | 85 | 94* | 76 | 61‡ | 76 | 83 | 12,265 |
| India | 43 | 64* | 46 | 46 | 42 | 45 | 35‡ | 51 | 3,157 |
| Pakistan | 60 | 79* | 38‡ | 76* | 45‡ | 44‡ | 29‡ | 57 | 425 |
| Poland | 38 | 37 | 34 | 63* | 49 | 47 | 30‡ | 41 | 4,128 |
| Ireland | 50 | 64 | 62 | 74* | 47‡ | 50 | 48‡ | 58 | 25,911 |
| Cyprus | 47 | 50 | 57 | 66* | 42‡ | 35‡ | 55 | 52 | 4,187 |

* 10% or more above the average.  † 1 in 25 sample of households.  ‡ 10% or more below the average.  Source: full Census analysis

(This table shows the proportion of persons living in the selected household groups (not the proportion of households) who occupied three rooms or less in the selected boroughs.)

TABLE 20
Persons per Room

| Number of persons per room | Percentage of persons in households with head born in England | Jamaica | Caribbean | India | Pakistan | Poland | Ireland | Cyprus |
|---|---|---|---|---|---|---|---|---|
| Over 1·5 | 8 | 53 | 63 | 24 | 29 | 9 | 32 | 41 |
| Over 1 up to 1·5 | 15 | 22 | 15 | 20 | 21 | 15 | 26 | 30 |
| 1 | 25 | 18 | 17 | 27 | 28 | 25 | 23 | 17 |
| 0·75 to under 1 | 15 | 3 | 2 | 10 | 6 | 15 | 7 | 6 |
| 0·5 to under 0·75 | 28 | 4 | 3 | 13 | 14 | 27 | 10 | 5 |
| Under 0·5 | 9 | * | * | 5 | 1 | 8 | 2 | 1 |
| | 100 | 100 | 100 | 100 | 100 | 100 | 100 | 100 |
| Number of persons | 26,288† | 24,987 | 14,849 | 6,130 | 740 | 10,136 | 44,268 | 8,013 |

* Less than 0·5%.  † 1 in 25 sample.  Source: full Census analysis

prove) that skin colour is not the most important consideration in this respect. The Irish and Cypriot households are apparently more overcrowded than the Indian and Pakistani.

Working on the basis of the average number of persons per room, the difference between the boroughs is not nearly so marked as it is when we consider the number of rooms occupied by households. The individual boroughs differ from the average by more than 10% in only one or two cases amongst Indian and Pakistani households, where the numbers are relatively small, and amongst the Polish households where there is quite a noticeable deviation, ranging from Stoke Newington, with 25% of the persons in Polish households living at a density in excess of one person to a room, to Deptford, with 46% living under such conditions. The Census figures themselves yield no explanation why these differences should occur, and speculation is futile without further field research into this particular question.

This point may be illustrated by considering in each separate borough and each different household group the proportion of persons living at a density greater than one person per room, as in Table 21. In general, the tables show that two factors work together: immigrants generally are more overcrowded than the English population; and when they live in particularly overcrowded boroughs they tend to be even more overcrowded. (The second of these factors does not apply to all immigrant groups.)

*Conditions of Houses*

The Census figures give no indication of the state of the houses in which the migrants live, and during the sample enquiry into Jamaican households throughout Britain careful attention was paid to reports from the visitors about the general conditions of the accommodation which they observed. As might be expected many conflicting reports were received which make generalization difficult, but it was noticeable that the majority of the reports indicated that, although crowded, the rooms visited were usually reasonably well furnished, and usually spotlessly clean. The reports concerning bad housing conditions generally related to the state of the house itself, or of the neighbourhood, whilst specifically saying that the tenants had done all that could be done in the situation to improve their housing conditions. Only in isolated cases was it implied

## TABLE 21

### Proportion of Persons living at a Density in excess of one Person per Room (Borough Analysis)
#### (per cent of persons)

| Households with head born in | Borough | | | | | | | Average of 7 boroughs | Number of persons living in the households |
| --- | --- | --- | --- | --- | --- | --- | --- | --- | --- |
| | Lambeth | Stoke Newington | Hackney | Paddington | Deptford | Battersea | Camberwell | | |
| England | 25 | 22 | 24 | 24 | 25 | 25 | 21 | 23 | 6,212* |
| Jamaica | 74 | 74 | 77 | 74 | 77 | 75 | 75 | 75 | 18,718 |
| Caribbean | 74 | 74 | 80 | 80 | 72 | 72 | 77 | 78 | 11,529 |
| India | 39 | 55 | 57 | 38 | 47 | 39 | 48 | 45 | 2,746 |
| Pakistan | 40 | 61 | 66 | 47 | 64 | 40 | 66 | 50 | 376 |
| Poland | 28 | 25 | 14 | 26 | 46 | 40 | 40 | 24 | 2,464 |
| Ireland | 56 | 54 | 60 | 61 | 53 | 53 | 54 | 57 | 25,261 |
| Cyprus | 66 | 74 | 76 | 65 | 61 | 68 | 71 | 70 | 5,622 |

\* 1 in 25 sample.

Source: full Census analysis

that the tenants were to be held responsible for the dirt and squalor with which they were surrounded. The bare statistics of overcrowding which have recently been examined take on a greater air of reality when a family is described as living in a tiny room where it is hardly possible to open the door when two people are inside. There were sufficient reports of this nature to cause concern, although it must always be remembered that the housing conditions from which the immigrants have departed in Jamaica and elsewhere in the Commonwealth may not be better than those they find in Britain, and might be a lot worse. Whilst the gloomy reports describing dark, smelly, badly decorated, under-furnished and overcrowded rooms were frequent, in many more cases a much brighter picture was painted. Just a few examples may be quoted by way of illustration:

Pleasant bedroom but most of life goes on in communal rooms. Very charming house in pleasant street, mostly white area.

Small house in good area—clean, well kept, not overcrowded. Garden well planted with flowers and vegetables.

House was shabby outside but clean and bright inside. Room was on second floor. Cooking-stove (shared) on landing.

A very well-cared-for house in a somewhat slummy area. By far the best in the street. Was being redecorated during my visit. Owner wanted to have it shown on television so that English people might realize that Jamaicans do not all live in squalor.

Reports such as these could be multiplied many times. It may be said without hesitation on the basis of the evidence collected during the survey that if Jamaican immigrants are in some cases living in squalor this is due to their own negligence in only a tiny minority of cases. The general picture is of a group of people contending with very adverse circumstances cheerfully trying to improve their position in life, and keeping themselves clean and tidy.

*Facilities*

From information collected during the Census we can form some judgement of housing standards by considering the extent to which basic amenities which many people in England simply take for granted are available either for the exclusive use of a household or on a shared basis. Each household during the Census was asked if they had the use, exclusively or otherwise, of: (1) a cold-water supply; (2) a hot-water supply; (3) a fixed bath; (4) a water closet.

A few preliminary definitions must first be made explicit.

(1) *Cold-water tap*. This refers to a tap within the building. It does not include a tap in an open yard or a public standpipe. If only the latter were available the enumerator was instructed to write 'None' on the Census schedule.

(2) *Hot-water tap*. This means water piped to any form of heating appliance which allowed hot water to be drawn from a tap within the building, e.g. a boiler, tank with immersion heater, geyser or sink heater.

(3) *Fixed bath*. This means a bath permanently installed with a waste pipe leading outside the building. It does not matter for this purpose whether there is water piped to it or whether the room where it is installed is used only as a bathroom or not.

(4) *Water closet*. This means any water closet emptying into a main sewer, septic tank or cesspool. It does not include a chemical closet or earth closet. It must be within the building or attached to it.

Our analysis sought to identify three separate situations: (a) where the houschold had the exclusive use of a particular facility; (b) where the household shared the facility with one or more other households; (c) where the household had no access to the particular facility.

We may examine first the households which had the *exclusive* use of *all four* of these facilities. Table 22 shows the proportion of households in the separate household groups which had the exclusive use of a cold-water tap, a hot-water tap, a fixed bath and a water closet.

It is clear that households headed by a person born in the West Indies are much less favourably placed than other household groups in the matter of household facilities. Only 8 % of the Caribbean households, as compared with 40 % of the English households, had the exclusive use of all four facilities. On the other hand households headed by a person born in Poland are slightly better off in this respect than those with an English-born head.

TABLE 22

*Exclusive Use of four Household Facilities*

| Households in which the head was born in | Per cent of households | Number of households |
|---|---|---|
| England | 40 | 9,604* |
| Jamaica | 12 | 7,597 |
| Caribbean | 8 | 5,211 |
| India | 35 | 2,190 |
| Pakistan | 25 | 269 |
| Poland | 43 | 3,793 |
| Ireland | 24 | 13,914 |
| Cyprus | 24 | 1,891 |

*Source:* full Census analysis
\* 1 in 25 sample.

(This table shows the proportion of households which had the exclusive use of a cold-water tap, hot-water tap, fixed bath and water closet.)

We can now consider the analysis of households in relation to their access to a cold-water tap showing separately where the households had the exclusive use, shared, or had no access to a cold-water tap within the building. Almost all the households had access to a cold-water tap within the building where they lived, but half of the West Indian households had to share this facility with other households, whereas only 4% of the English households did so. The West Indian households are again in the least favourable position, although it is perhaps as well to remember that they are no worse off in this respect in England than many of them were at home in the West Indies, where a cold-water tap within the building is still something of a luxury, particularly in the rural areas. Almost all the Indian and Pakistani households had the exclusive use of a cold-water tap whilst all the other groups, apart from West Indians, record over 80% with this exclusive facility (Table 23).

The situation is very different when we look at access to a hot-water supply. It is perhaps somewhat surprising to find from Table 24 that where households are headed by persons born in India, Pakistan or Poland, each category has 60% or more of the households with the exclusive use of a hot-water tap. These are therefore better placed than the English households, who record only 55% with this exclusive facility. It is equally surprising to find that 42% of the English households had no access to a hot-water tap, whilst only a quarter of the

## TABLE 23

*Access to a Cold-Water Tap (per cent of households)*

| Households headed by a person born in | Exclusive use | Shared | No access |
|---|---|---|---|
| England | 96 | 4 | * |
| Jamaica | 50 | 49 | * |
| Caribbean | 54 | 46 | * |
| India | 90 | 10 | * |
| Pakistan | 85 | 15 | * |
| Poland | 93 | 7 | * |
| Ireland | 86 | 14 | * |
| Cyprus | 86 | 14 | * |

*Source:* full Census analysis

* Less than 0·5%.

(The number of households is identical with that in Table 22.)

## TABLE 24

*Access to a Hot-Water Tap (per cent of households)*

| Households headed by a person born in | Exclusive use | Shared | No access |
|---|---|---|---|
| England | 55 | 3 | 42 |
| Jamaica | 21 | 27 | 52 |
| Caribbean | 19 | 22 | 59 |
| India | 65 | 12 | 23 |
| Pakistan | 60 | 15 | 25 |
| Poland | 63 | 8 | 29 |
| Ireland | 38 | 9 | 53 |
| Cyprus | 44 | 9 | 47 |

*Source:* full Census analysis

Indian and Pakistani households are so deprived. Perhaps this may to some extent be explained by the importance normally attached to cleanliness within Indian and Pakistani society. As before, the West Indians are relatively badly placed, but they are not noticeably worse off than the Irish or Cypriot households. In all these cases over 45% of the households had no access at all to a hot-water tap, a proportion that rises to 59% in the case of the Caribbean households.

The exclusive use of a fixed bath is a luxury which not even half the households in the most favoured group enjoyed. In the case of Caribbean households, hardly more than one household in ten had this facility exclusively, whilst almost one Caribbean, Irish and Cypriot household in three had no access at all to a fixed bath at home, but this proportion is also recorded in the case of English households, who are much worse off than Indian, Pakistani and Polish households in this respect (Table 25).

TABLE 25

*Access to a Fixed Bath (per cent of households)*

| Households headed by a person born in | Exclusive use | Shared | No access |
|---|---|---|---|
| England | 47 | 16 | 37 |
| Jamaica | 19 | 55 | 25 |
| Caribbean | 14 | 54 | 32 |
| India | 41 | 46 | 13 |
| Pakistan | 32 | 51 | 17 |
| Poland | 49 | 37 | 14 |
| Ireland | 31 | 32 | 37 |
| Cyprus | 33 | 31 | 36 |

*Source:* full Census analysis

Almost all the households had some access to a water closet, the least favourably placed being those headed by the Cypriot group, where 3% of the households had no access to a water closet. On the other hand the proportion of households with the exclusive use of this facility varies considerably as between the different household groups. 70% of the 'English' and 63% of the 'Polish' households have the exclusive use of a water closet, whereas four out of five 'Caribbean' households have to share one with at least one other household. The Jamaican households are slightly better off than the Caribbean, but not much. About half the Indian, Pakistani, Irish and Cypriot households share the use of a water closet (Table 26).

The attitude which people adopt towards their housing conditions, and their general approach towards the society in which they live, are conditioned to some extent by their tenure of the property. A man who buys a house in an area usually has some intention of settling there for some time and his relationship with the wider community is likely to be affected by his decision. Similarly a family living in a subsidized council house is normally less likely to move once it has secured possession, perhaps after waiting for years on a housing list. On the other

## TABLE 26

*Access to a Water Closet (per cent of households)*

| Households headed by a person born in | Exclusive use | Shared | No access |
|---|---|---|---|
| England | 70 | 29 | 1 |
| Jamaica | 26 | 72 | 1 |
| Caribbean | 19 | 80 | 1 |
| India | 49 | 50 | 1 |
| Pakistan | 39 | 59 | 2 |
| Poland | 63 | 36 | 1 |
| Ireland | 48 | 50 | 2 |
| Cyprus | 48 | 49 | 3 |

*Source:* full Census analysis

hand a person paying a high rent for a single furnished room is likely to be much more mobile, with only tenuous roots in the district. These are, of course, generalizations to which many exceptions can be found, but whatever the precise effect tenure may have on mobility and the process of integration it is clearly a factor which cannot be ignored.

The Census material for the seven boroughs was analysed for the eight household groups according to the tenure of property, as follows:

(1) Owner-occupiers, including purchasers by mortgage. As well as freeholders this category included households which occupied their accommodation on a lease which was originally granted for more than twenty-one years or had been extended for more than twenty-one years. If the accommodation was held on a shorter lease it should have been included in one of the other categories.

(2) Tenants who hold property by renting it with a farm, shop or other business premises.

(3) Tenants who hold property by virtue of employment. A household should have been included in this category if the accommodation was provided in connection with the employment of a member of the household and would cease to be provided after the employment came to an end. The tied cottage and the caretaker's flat were the examples cited on the schedule; other examples are accommodation provided by a firm for its employees, that provided by the police for police officers and the vicarage. This category did not include cases where an

employer obtained the accommodation for an employee, without any conditions as to employment.

(4) Tenants who hold property by renting it from the council or New Town Corporation.

(5) Tenants who hold property by renting it privately from another person as landlord. The household had to specify whether the accommodation was rented furnished or unfurnished.

(6) Tenants who hold property in some other way: details to be provided.

Once the different household groups had been classified in this way in the seven boroughs it was possible to examine (a) the number of *households* in each tenure category; (b) the number of *persons* living in the households in each tenure category; and (c) the number of *rooms* occupied by households in each tenure category.

It makes a great deal of difference which basis is taken. If we take as an example the category of households with a head born in Jamaica in all seven boroughs considered together, we find that 61% of the *households* were renting furnished accommodation. If we perform a different calculation we find that 39% of the *rooms* occupied by those households were rented furnished. Yet again we find that 45% of the *persons* living in those households were classified in the 'renting furnished' category. As a further example, we may consider the households headed by a person born in the Caribbean. It transpires that 14% of the households were renting unfurnished accommodation, 18% of the rooms occupied by those households were in the 'renting unfurnished' category, as were 16% of the persons living in those households. It turns out, in most cases, that a proportion calculated on the basis of persons lies between the proportion calculated on the basis of households and that on the basis of rooms. There is no 'correct' way of doing it—in this study the summary figures over the seven boroughs are given on each of these bases. A word of warning should be given about the interpretation of these specific figures: they cannot with confidence be assumed to give an indication of the position throughout London and certainly not throughout Britain. The boroughs included in the present sample were selected because they contained a high proportion of a particular group of immigrants who were the main focus of this particular study.

## TABLE 27

### Analysis of Property Tenure (per cent)

#### (a) HOUSEHOLDS

| Tenure | English | Jamaican | Caribbean excluding Jamaican | Indian | Pakistani | Polish | Irish | Cypriot |
|---|---|---|---|---|---|---|---|---|
| Owner-occupiers | 13 | 25 | 9 | 16 | 18 | 33 | 8 | 34 |
| Renting furnished | 7 | 61 | 75 | 48 | 58 | 18 | 34 | 28 |
| Renting unfurnished | 53 | 12 | 14 | 26 | 16 | 35 | 40 | 30 |
| Renting from Council | 24 | 1 | 1 | 7 | 5 | 13 | 15 | 6 |
| Other | 3 | 1 | 1 | 3 | 3 | 1 | 3 | 2 |
| | 100 | 100 | 100 | 100 | 100 | 100 | 100 | 100 |
| Number of households | 9,604* | 7,597 | 5,211 | 2,190 | 269 | 3,793 | 13,914 | 1,891 |

#### (b) PERSONS

| Tenure | English | Jamaican | Caribbean excluding Jamaican | Indian | Pakistani | Polish | Irish | Cypriot |
|---|---|---|---|---|---|---|---|---|
| Owner-occupiers | 14 | 40 | 17 | 24 | 33 | 41 | 11 | 42 |
| Renting furnished | 5 | 45 | 66 | 35 | 39 | 12 | 25 | 20 |
| Renting unfurnished | 50 | 13 | 16 | 28 | 17 | 32 | 42 | 29 |
| Renting from Council | 28 | 1 | 1 | 10 | 8 | 14 | 19 | 7 |
| Other | 3 | 1 | † | 3 | 4 | 1 | 3 | 2 |
| | 100 | 100 | 100 | 100 | 100 | 100 | 100 | 100 |
| Number of persons | 26,288* | 24,987 | 14,849 | 6,130 | 740 | 10,136 | 44,268 | 8,013 |

#### (c) ROOMS

| Tenure | English | Jamaican | Caribbean excluding Jamaican | Indian | Pakistani | Polish | Irish | Cypriot |
|---|---|---|---|---|---|---|---|---|
| Owner-occupiers | 18 | 45 | 21 | 29 | 34 | 45 | 14 | 45 |
| Renting furnished | 4 | 39 | 60 | 28 | 36 | 8 | 21 | 16 |
| Renting unfurnished | 52 | 14 | 18 | 31 | 20 | 33 | 43 | 29 |
| Renting from Council | 23 | 2 | 1 | 9 | 7 | 13 | 19 | 7 |
| Other | 3 | † | † | 3 | 3 | 1 | 3 | 3 |
| | 100 | 100 | 100 | 100 | 100 | 100 | 100 | 100 |
| Number of rooms | 35,692* | 17,254 | 9,261 | 6,372 | 674 | 13,507 | 5,713 | 6,196 |

\* 1 in 25 sample of English households.  † Less than 0.5%.  Source: full Census analysis

They cannot be taken as 'typical' of London in any way—on the contrary they are probably quite dissimilar from the London boroughs in the outer ring of the county (Table 27).

Owner-occupation is probably the most favoured of the tenure possibilities amongst all groups of the community, although renting unfurnished accommodation (provided the rents are controlled by statute) may be not less attractive financially. A tenant in a controlled house has security of tenure, usually an artificially low rental, and he can endeavour to have maintenance work carried out by the landlord. The least favourable position is that of the tenant who occupies furnished premises. Here the rents are usually high and there is little or no security of tenure. Council tenants are a privileged group usually living in accommodation in relatively good condition, with security of tenure and at a subsidized rental.

Among English households, 53% rent unfurnished from private landlords, one household in four (24%) from the council. Relatively few of the 'English' households (13%) are in the owner-occupier class. Furthermore only 7% of the households, (5% of the persons and 4% of the rooms) are rented on a furnished basis. The contrast with the group of households headed by a person born in the Caribbean area is startling. In this case 75% of the households rent furnished which means that high rents are certainly being extracted from the tenants. Hardly any of the 'Caribbean' group rent from the council; nor do many Jamaican, Indian, Pakistani or Cypriot households. This fact does not indicate that any form of conscious racial discrimination is being practised in the matter of allocating council houses. The explanation for the different proportions housed by the public authorities is more a matter of time, and of how long families have been on the waiting list.

Jamaicans are much more inclined to be home-owners than the Caribbeans, whether by design or necessity, for 25% of the households (40% of the persons, 45% of the rooms) in 'Jamaican households are owner-occupied. Over half the households headed by a person born in Ireland (61% of the persons, 62% of the rooms) are either renting unfurnished or from the council. Similarly a high proportion (48% households, 46% persons, 46% rooms) in the 'Polish' households seem to be favourably placed so far as renting is concerned. It does not seem possible to doubt, when these statistics are examined, that households with an English-born head have an overwhelming advantage over any immigrant group in the housing field with greater security of tenure and possibly a lower level of rent. The households headed by a white immigrant (from Poland or Ireland) are reasonably well placed, households headed by an Indian or Pakistani come next, with the Jamaican and Caribbean households in the worst position of all.

The discussion on property tenure has so far concerned the seven London boroughs taken together. The question may reasonably be asked whether the boroughs differ a great deal in this respect. It is impossible to reproduce here all the statistics which have been assembled on this point, but the discussion

TABLE 28

*Tenure of Jamaican Households (Borough Analysis)*
*(per cent of persons)*

| Tenure | Lambeth | Stoke Newington | Hackney | Paddington | Deptford | Battersea | Camberwell | Average |
|---|---|---|---|---|---|---|---|---|
| | | | | Borough | | | | |
| Owner-occupier | 38 | 36 | 34 | 27 | 55 | 53 | 49 | 40 |
| Renting furnished | 49 | 45 | 48 | 57 | 34 | 35 | 36 | 45 |
| Renting unfurnished | 11 | 19 | 18 | 15 | 10 | 10 | 12 | 13 |
| Renting from Council | 2 | * | 1 | 1 | 1 | 1 | 2 | 1 |
| Other | * | * | * | * | 1 | * | 1 | 1 |
| | 100 | 100 | 100 | 100 | 100 | 100 | 100 | 100 |
| Number of persons | 9,111 | 1,538 | 4,349 | 2,026 | 1,642 | 2,658 | 3,663 | 24,987 |

*Source:* full Census analysis

* Less than 0·5%.

(This table shows the proportion of persons living in households headed by a person born in Jamaica in each of the main tenure categories.)

may be concluded by giving the details recorded for the households headed by Jamaicans in each of the boroughs separately, basing the analysis on the proportion of persons living in the household, not on the proportion of households or the proportion of rooms. It would appear that a far greater proportion of persons living in Jamaican households in Paddington are renting their accommodation furnished than anywhere else in the seven boroughs: 57% was the proportion recorded in Paddington as compared with an average of 45% and the low level of 34% in Deptford. In the latter borough 55% of the persons living in Jamaican households are in owner-occupied premises, whilst in Paddington only 27% are so recorded. Never more than 2% live in council houses and usually the proportion is nearer 1% (Table 28).

*Shared Dwellings*

For Census purposes all households are regarded as living in 'dwellings' which may be occupied exclusively by one household or may be shared with one or more other households. A 'dwelling' is defined as a building or part of a building which provides separate living-quarters. A dwelling is normally a private dwelling-house, flat or maisonette with a front door of its own. Where houses or other buildings have been adapted to provide residential accommodation in smaller units, these smaller units are regarded as dwellings if they are structurally separate. That is, if such a unit has a separate front door to the street and is self-contained (separated from the rest of the building by a wall or solid partition), then it is counted as a dwelling. When access to such a unit is through part of the building, it is counted as a dwelling only if access to the main door is gained by means of a common staircase or landing. If it can only be reached through the quarters occupied or normally occupied by another household (including a hall) it is not counted as a dwelling. For such a unit to count as a dwelling it also must be possible to move between its rooms internally without making use of the common staircase or landing, and normally there is one door of the unit opening on the common internal part of the building (disregarding access to shop or office portions of the building).

Normally a dwelling has more than one living-room in addition to kitchen and bathroom, but one-room flats are counted as dwellings if they meet the conditions set out above, provided that they either include a separate kitchenette or have a cooking-stove in the room and a separate bathroom and water closet. Bed-sitting-rooms (sometimes called one-room flatlets) are not counted as separate dwellings. The whole of the quarters occupied or normally occupied by households (that is,

the household space) within any building had to be included by
the Census enumerator in one or other of the dwellings within
it. If the building was arranged in such a way that there was no
reasonable way of dividing it into dwellings, the whole building
was regarded as a single dwelling. In pursuing the present investigation the computer was instructed to select households,
not dwellings, and it was necessary to make some adjustment
of the data when two or more households with heads of different
birthplace shared a single dwelling.[1]

Households are categorized by country of origin and the
number in each borough who were reported to be sharing a
dwelling is expressed as a proportion of all households in that
particular category in that borough. This is done in Table 29
which shows, for example, that 79 % of the households in Lambeth who were headed by a person born in Jamaica shared a
dwelling with at least one other household, whilst 89 % of the
Jamaican households in Hackney and 59 % of the Jamaican
households in Camberwell did so.

Looking at the position in the seven boroughs as a whole, we
observe that households headed by a person born in England
share a dwelling only to the extent of about one household in
three. It must be remembered that the boroughs included in
this analysis are amongst the least affluent of London as a whole.
These 'English' households are very much better off than those
in which the head was born in the Caribbean area—here more
than four households in five share a dwelling. The households
with a Jamaican head are slightly better off—here about three
households in four share a dwelling. In the case of households
headed by persons born in India, Pakistan, Ireland and Cyprus,
roughly one household in two shares a dwelling. The households headed by a person born in Poland are a lot better off
again but still noticeably less favourably placed than the
'English' households in this respect.

[1] The method used was that every household was made to appear to be the first
household in a dwelling unless the immediately preceding household had a 'head'
with the same birthplace as the 'head' of the household then being considered. The
general effect of this is that if a household falling in the sample shares a dwelling
with a household of which the 'head' was not born in the same country, the household is treated as though it occupied the whole of the dwelling and the dwelling size
related only to the parts of the dwelling occupied by the households in the sample
and not necessarily to the whole dwelling. This somewhat awkward method was
necessitated by technical considerations arising from the computer programme and
data organization.

TABLE 29

*Households in Shared Dwellings (per cent of households)*

| Head of household born in | Lam- beth | Stoke Newing- ton | Hackney | Padding- ton | Dept- ford | Batter- sea | Camber- well | Seven boroughs |
|---|---|---|---|---|---|---|---|---|
| England | 26 | 25 | 44 | 41 | 29 | 36 | 16 | 30 |
| Jamaica | 79 | 69 | 89 | 78 | 65 | 72 | 59 | 76 |
| Caribbean | 77 | 67 | 91 | 87 | 75 | 73 | 66 | 82 |
| India | 35 | 57 | 74 | 62 | 37 | 50 | 23 | 52 |
| Pakistan | 50 | 65 | 63 | 65 | 44 | 45 | 27 | 57 |
| Poland | 37 | 34 | 47 | 51 | 36 | 61 | 32 | 45 |
| Ireland | 41 | 48 | 68 | 63 | 36 | 49 | 24 | 50 |
| Cyprus | 45 | 51 | 72 | 59 | 32 | 45 | 32 | 51 |

*Source:* full Census analysis

(The table records the proportion of households sharing a dwelling with one or more other households.)

There are variations between the boroughs which are too large to be ignored. Paddington again stands out as the borough which seems to be worse than any of the others. In every single household category the proportion of households sharing a dwelling in Paddington is higher than the average, although a similar statement can also be made for Hackney. On the other hand Deptford and Camberwell are considerably lower than the average in each household category, and Lambeth exceeds it only in Jamaican households.

This is as far as the analysis of Census figures can take us, and it must be remembered that the extent to which households share dwellings is a function of the size of households, the size of dwellings and household incomes. At one time Paddington, which appears to show up rather badly in the above table, was a fashionable area of London with large houses now given over to tenements. It may well be that dwellings in Paddington are larger than dwellings in, say, Battersea and it is therefore more likely that households will share them. When these statistics are compared with those presented in Table 21 (see above, page 45), which records the proportion of persons living in excess of one person per room, we see that the difference between Paddington and the average of the seven boroughs is not so great. Furthermore if it were to be true (we have no statistical evidence on this point at all) that *rooms* are larger in Paddington than elsewhere, despite all the appearances to the contrary Paddington may not be so much more crowded than the other boroughs.

## Chapter IV

## EMPLOYMENT

THE question of the employment of immigrants is potentially one of the most explosive elements in the whole complex of relationships between the native and immigrant populations in Britain today. Competition for housing is certainly acute, but it can be solved or at least concealed, in the short run, by overcrowding. Competition for jobs is even more fundamental a matter, for access to the means of earning a livelihood is basic to survival. Since the end of the second World War, Britain has enjoyed a period of virtually full employment—her general unemployment rate has been minimal (apart from the occasional seasonal upsurge) and there has been an almost constant labour shortage in some sectors of the economy in some geographical areas (for instance, the hospital services, and public transport services in London). It is the existence of these pockets of labour shortage which the local inhabitants have been reluctant to overcome which has led in some measure to the tapping of new sources of immigrant labour in the tropical Commonwealth.

So long as full employment continues, and so long as there are parts of the economic system which the English and white immigrants are, in the main, content to leave to coloured labour, there is no reason to expect that any particularly serious problems need arise. The difficulties begin when the coloured immigrants themselves want to abandon the unattractive jobs and seek better opportunities elsewhere in the economy, particularly when they claim the right to work in skilled trades where strong craft trade unions operate. Trouble also begins when coloured workers, by virtue of length of employment and satisfactory service, find themselves eligible for supervisory jobs. If the coloured workers are promoted to supervisory jobs, particularly if they are given authority over white workers, difficulties can arise; if they are refused promotion because the management is fearful of opposition from the white employees the coloured workers, quite justifiably, may assert the existence of racial discrimination in industry. If the time ever comes when a much higher level of unemployment, extending over a prolonged period, should recur in Britain, then it may be expected that the white population will want to move back into those sectors of the economy which they had previously abandoned as unattractive. If they then find the coloured immigrants firmly entrenched, there is bound to be a great political outcry and growing pressures on managements, if not to replace existing coloured employees by whites, at any rate to pursue a racially discriminatory policy when recruiting new staff or replacing those who leave. The pressure on the Government further to restrict immigration by exercising its powers under the Commonwealth Immigrants Act will considerably increase.[1]

In the first two years following the start of controls under the Commonwealth Immigrants Act 718,930 persons subject to the controls entered Britain, 601,272 embarked, leaving a net inflow of 117,658. Of these 50% of the persons admitted were men, 38% were women and 11% were children. Of the embarkations 52% were men, 39% were women and 9% were children.

The quarterly record since July 1962 has been summarized in Table 3, from which it is clear that the statistics are beginning to display a markedly seasonal variation, rising sharply in the summer and falling in the winter. One need go no further than refer to the rigours of the English winter to seek an explanation, for an analysis of the first eighteen months of the operation of the Act reveals that almost half (47%) of the persons admitted were classified as visitors for three months or less, whilst 19% were persons returning to the United Kingdom from temporary absence abroad. Five further categories are distinguished in the official statistics, each of which accounts for 6 to 7% of the total admissions. These are: (a) visitors for more than three months; (b) students; (c) holders of Ministry of Labour vouchers; (d) dependants accompanying or coming to join the head of the household.

Other categories, amounting to less than 2% of the total admissions, are diplomats and officials with their dependants, persons joining crews of ships or aircraft and persons coming for settlement not included elsewhere.[2]

[1] These words were written before the White Paper appeared in August 1965.
[2] In the House of Commons on 17 November 1964, Sir Frank Soskice, the Home

Out of the total net inflow recorded during the two years, from July 1962 84% came from seven countries in the Commonwealth. India provided almost one in four (24%), Pakistan almost one in five (19%), Nigeria, Canada and Jamaica each provided about one in ten (Nigeria 12%, Canada 11%, Jamaica 9%). The number of employment vouchers issued by the Ministry of Labour dropped sharply in the second half of the second year. In the first year vouchers were being issued at an average rate of 3,729 per month. In the first half of the second year (that is, July to December 1963), the average monthly issue was 3,623, but in the first half of 1964 this figure fell to 1,737. In the first year 27% of the applicants were issued with vouchers, as compared with 13% the second year. By the end of the second year the Ministry of Labour had built up a backlog of 339,949 applications still awaiting the issue of vouchers. This means that 82% of the applicants for vouchers were still on the waiting list.

One of the best ways to assess the extent to which immigrant labour has contributed to the British labour force is to examine the statistics prepared by the Ministry of Pensions and National Insurance relating to the number of persons who joined the national insurance scheme in a given period.[1] The official statistics we shall now consider include all immigrants from the British Commonwealth, or aliens, who became new entrants into the national insurance scheme in Great Britain (as distinct from the United Kingdom) in the period 1956 to 1963. Nonworking dependants of immigrants are excluded from the statistics, nor do they include anyone (for instance a retired person) who falls outside the scope of the National Insurance Acts. Slight inaccuracies due to time-lags and non-compliance with the law are not likely to be significant. The figures include people, mainly aliens, who represent only short-term additions

Secretary, said that 31,000 immigrants could not be accounted for. They had presumably been admitted as visitors but had found employment. He was speaking in the debate on the Expiring Laws Continuation Act extending existing controls on Commonwealth immigration for a further year.

[1] Grateful acknowledgement is made to the officials of the Ministry of Pensions and National Insurance who willingly co-operated in this study by making figures available to the author, with lucid explanations. Earlier figures were first published and discussed in an article on 'Immigration and Unemployment in the U.K.', *British Journal of Industrial Relations*, Vol. 1, No. 1. The Ministry officials are not in any way responsible for the presentation of, or commentary on, the raw data they have supplied.

to the manpower of Britain (such as seasonal workers, student employees, or entertainers). A substantial number of aliens granted permits for employment in Great Britain return home within a year. Re-entrants to the national insurance scheme are excluded throughout.

The main difficulty in using these statistics, for present purposes, is that they record only *applicants* for insurance. No information is available concerning people *leaving* the national insurance scheme. Whilst it may appear somewhat ungracious to complain of the lack of such statistics, when so much trouble is taken to prepare the first set, one cannot but regret that it has not been possible for the Ministry of Pensions and National Insurance to prepare statistics showing the categories of overseas people who leave the national insurance scheme. There are undoubtedly technical difficulties involved, and the exercise may not now be considered worth while in view of the new sources of statistics which have appeared under the Commonwealth Immigrants Act.

In this period, 1956 to 1963 inclusive, just over one and a quarter million immigrants entered the national insurance scheme in Britain for the first time. Of these, 43% came from the British Commonwealth, 29% from the Irish Republic and 28% were aliens.[1] If we examine each year separately, as in Table 30, we observe that the total number of new entrants fell by nearly 17% from 1956 to 1958, rose by 65% in the period 1959 to 1961, and fell by 38% in the period 1962 to 1963. Although this is not demonstrated by the figures themselves, there can be little doubt that the sharp contraction following 1961 was due in large measure to the operation of the Commonwealth Immigrants Act. Up to 1962 the proportion of new entrants arriving from the British Commonwealth, although not showing a steady trend, tended to increase from 38% in 1956 to 55% in 1962. In 1963 the proportion fell sharply to 46%. The proportion of new arrivals from the Irish Republic, although again not steady in different years, tended to contract from 34% to 36% in 1956–9, to 23% in 1963. From 1956 to 1961 the proportion of new entrants from foreign countries ranged from 28% to 35%. In 1960–1 the proportion was down to 25%. In 1963 it had risen to 31%. These figures are not sufficient to record a trend, but they

[1] Persons from South Africa are regarded as 'aliens' throughout although that country was a member of the British Commonwealth for part of that period.

suggest that the first effect of the Commonwealth Immigrants Act has been to increase the proportion of aliens at the expense of Commonwealth citizens, but it will be necessary to observe these statistics over the next year or two to decide whether this is fair comment or rash generalization.

TABLE 30

*Persons arriving from Overseas applying for
National Insurance Cards, 1956–63*

| Year | Total applicants | British Commonwealth | Per cent Irish Republic | Foreigners |
|------|------------------|----------------------|-------------------------|------------|
| 1956 | 167,488 | 38 | 34 | 28 |
| 1957 | 168,416 | 30 | 35 | 35 |
| 1958 | 139,060 | 34 | 34 | 31 |
| 1959 | 142,996 | 35 | 36 | 29 |
| 1960 | 192,091 | 45 | 30 | 25 |
| 1961 | 229,389 | 51 | 23 | 25 |
| 1962 | 199,023 | 55 | 19 | 26 |
| 1963 | 142,322 | 46 | 23 | 31 |
| 1956– 63 | 1,380,785 | 43 | 29 | 28 |

*Source:* Ministry of Pensions and National Insurance

The majority (39%) of the new entrants to the national insurance scheme in the period 1956–63 came from the Caribbean area, the great majority coming from the West Indian islands. The next largest contingent (28%) came from Asia, dominated by India and Pakistan. From the temperate Commonwealth came 21% of the new entrants, with Australia in the lead, followed by Canada, Cyprus and New Zealand, in that order. Africa and the rest of the Commonwealth provided only 12%. The predominant position of the Irish Republic among the non-Commonwealth new arrivals has already been noted, and if we exclude that country it turns out that 82% of the alien new entrants came from Europe—particularly the Federal Republic of Germany (17%), Italy (17%), Spain (10%), Switzerland (9%) and France (7%). The only other country which calls for special mention outside Europe is the Union of South Africa, which provided just under 8%. Of the non-Commonwealth new entrants, the U.S.A. provided only 4% (Table 31 on pages 66–67).

At the 1961 Census one person in every ten was asked whether or not he had been in employment during the week ending Saturday, 22 April 1961. If he was away from work because of holidays, sickness, strike or other reasons, he was regarded as being in employment. 'Employment' included any service in the armed forces and also jobs at which a person worked for only a few hours a week, but did not include persons at school or university full-time during term, even if they worked during the holidays. All employed persons were asked to state their employers' names and business, and they were also asked to state their own occupation. As the volume of information to be scanned by the computer was so much less than in the full Census—being based on a 10% sample, not the whole population—it was possible for all the schedules in each of the twenty-eight metropolitan boroughs (that is, covering approximately 10% of the population of London) to be examined in the course of the present enquiry and a new classification to be made on the basis of the stated birthplace of the respondent. The classification, it will be observed, does not relate to households but to individuals, and includes persons who stated they were born in Jamaica, the Caribbean other than Jamaica, India, Pakistan, Poland, Cyprus and Ireland. In the case of persons who stated that they were born in England one name was selected at random out of every twenty-five.

The persons in the sample, separately for each sex in each of the metropolitan boroughs, could then be divided into two groups: (a) 'economically active'; and (b) 'not economically active'. Persons in the 'economically active' groups could then be further subdivided according to whether they were in employment or out of employment in the week ending 22 April 1961. The 'not economically active' group included all children under the age of fifteen years, retired persons, housewives, students and similar groups. Table 32 (page 68) shows the aggregate position for all the twenty-eight metropolitan boroughs: once again, the City of London is excluded throughout. Among all the immigrant groups a substantially higher proportion of males are 'economically active' than among the English-born. The difference is due, presumably, to the higher proportion of English-born males who are receiving some form of higher education after the age of fifteen and the higher proportion of retired persons. (It will be observed that both employed and unemployed are regarded as 'economically active'; the rate of unemployment, to which more attention will be given in the subsequent chapter, has nothing to do with these proportions.) In the case of females the contrast between the English-born and those born in Jamaica and the rest of the Caribbean is quite striking. Just over one English-born woman in three was classified as 'economically active', whilst almost two out of three

TABLE 31

*Geographical Analysis of New Entrants to the Labour Force, 1956–63*

(a) COMMONWEALTH

| | Region | Country total | Regional total |
|---|---|---|---|
| (1) | *British Isles* | | |
| | Channel Islands | 3,651 | 3,651 |
| (2) | *Temperate* | | |
| | Australia | 46,496 | |
| | Canada | 21,346 | |
| | Cyprus | 28,967 | |
| | New Zealand | 17,946 | |
| | Malta | 7,095 | |
| | Gibraltar | 1,927 | |
| | | | 123,786 |
| (3) | *Asia* | | |
| | Pakistan | 67,882 | |
| | India | 61,777 | |
| | Malaysia* | 11,327 | |
| | Hong Kong | 12,236 | |
| | Ceylon | 5,764 | |
| | Aden | 3,966 | |
| | Persian Gulf States | 512 | |
| | | | 163,464 |
| (4) | *Caribbean* | | |
| | West Indian Islands | 218,907 | |
| | British Guiana | 13,936 | |
| | British Honduras | 241 | |
| | | | 233,084 |
| (5) | *Africa* | | |
| | West Africa | 38,210 | |
| | East Africa | 16,330 | |
| | Central Africa† | 3,466 | |
| | | | 58,006 |
| (6) | *Rest of Commonwealth* | 8,464 | 8,464 |
| | *Total Commonwealth:* | | 590,455 |

* Malaya, Singapore, Sarawak, North Borneo.
† Nyasaland, Southern Rhodesia, Zambia.

TABLE 31 (cont.)

| (b) NON-COMMONWEALTH | | |
|---|---|---|
| Region | Country total | Regional total |
| (1) Ireland | 397,047 | 397,047 |
| (2) Europe | | |
| Germany (Federal Republic) | 67,119 | |
| Italy | 66,445 | |
| Spain | 37,444 | |
| Switzerland | 35,750 | |
| France | 25,992 | |
| Hungary | 17,166 | |
| Netherlands | 13,598 | |
| Denmark | 12,093 | |
| Austria | 9,523 | |
| Sweden | 7,525 | |
| Rest of Europe | 29,480 | |
| | | 322,135 |
| (3) Africa | | |
| Union of South Africa | 29,688 | |
| Rest of Africa | 8,707 | |
| | | 38,395 |
| (4) America | | |
| United States of America | 16,784 | |
| Rest of America | 3,583 | |
| | | 20,367 |
| (5) Asia (including Middle and Far East) | 12,386 | 12,386 |
| Total Non-Commonwealth: | | 790,330 |
| Total World: | | 1,380,785 |

Source: Ministry of Pensions and National Insurance

of the women born in the West Indies fell into this category. To some extent the longer education and larger numbers in the higher age groups affect the position, but the main difference is probably due to the fact that more English women stay at home as housewives than do West Indian women, many of whom have left their children behind in the West Indies, or with baby-sitters, and go out to work to support them. On the other hand, the proportion of women born in Pakistan, Poland and Cyprus who are not economically active is similar to that of the English. Women born in India and Ireland are in an intermediate position: they have a higher proportion in the economically active category than the English but less than the West Indians.

All the individuals included in the 10% sample of the population were asked to give their occupation (but useful information is available only for males). For each separate birthplace group the economically active males were classified into six

## TABLE 32

### Employment

#### (a) MALES

| Birthplace | Persons in sample (1) | In employ (2) | Out of employ (3) | Econ. active (4) =(2)+(3) | % Econ. active (4) as % of (1) |
|---|---|---|---|---|---|
| England | 4,934 | 3,134 | 102 | 3,236 | 66 |
| Jamaica | 1,575 | 1,284 | 103 | 1,387 | 88 |
| Caribbean | 1,450 | 1,171 | 75 | 1,246 | 86 |
| India | 1,411 | 1,011 | 47 | 1,058 | 75 |
| Pakistan | 270 | 194 | 11 | 205 | 76 |
| Poland | 1,305 | 1,084 | 47 | 1,131 | 87 |
| Ireland | 6,662 | 5,689 | 288 | 5,977 | 90 |
| Cyprus | 1,138 | 819 | 50 | 869 | 76 |

#### (b) FEMALES

| Birthplace | Persons in sample (1) | In employ (2) | Out of employ (3) | Econ. active (4) =(2)+(3) | % Econ. active (4) as % of (1) |
|---|---|---|---|---|---|
| England | 5,457 | 2,084 | 54 | 2,138 | 39 |
| Jamaica | 1,417 | 824 | 60 | 884 | 62 |
| Caribbean | 1,150 | 635 | 52 | 687 | 60 |
| India | 1,118 | 521 | 20 | 541 | 48 |
| Pakistan | 91 | 28 | — | 28 | 31 |
| Poland | 866 | 296 | 20 | 316 | 36 |
| Ireland | 7,456 | 3,883 | 103 | 3,986 | 53 |
| Cyprus | 925 | 345 | 9 | 354 | 38 |

*Source:* 10% Census analysis

broad occupational categories, which were a condensation of the principal occupational categories listed in the Standard Occupational Classification of 1960. The six groups are defined as follows and relate to the main categories of the Standard Classification.

| Category No. | Title | S.O.C. categories included | Examples of occupations included |
|---|---|---|---|
| 1. | Professional | 3, 4 | Medical practitioners, judges, non-manual professional employees. |
| 2. | Employers and managers | 1, 2, 13 | Hotel keepers, garage proprietors, restaurateurs, valets, street vendors, fishermen, launderers, jewellery manufacturers—provided they are self-employed with employees. |
| 3. | Foremen. Skilled manual. Own account (other than professional) | 8, 9 12 14, | Foremen and supervisors. Skilled occupations. Partly skilled occupations. Pilots, publicans, typists, farmers. Self-employed *without* employees. |

| 4. | Non-manual | 5, 6 | Nurses, laboratory assistants, shop salesmen, telegraph operators, draughtsmen, caretakers, guards. |
| 5. | Personal Service. Semi-skilled manual and agriculture | 7,10,15 | Barmen, maids, cooks, hairdressers, chimney-sweeps, agricultural workers. |
| 6. | Unskilled manual. Armed Forces and persons with inadequately described occupations | 11, 16, 17 | Unskilled manual employees. Members of Armed Forces. Persons with inadequately described occupations. |

In general terms, these six categories are in name-order of prestige and of social class, so that the most desirable are numbers 1 and 2, and the least desirable are numbers 5 and 6.

Table 33 overleaf shows the occupational distribution of males according to their places of origin. In categories 5 and 6 (the lowest in terms of status) are proportionately more Jamaicans, Caribbeans, Pakistanis and Cypriots than in categories 1 and 2. The two West Indian groups share with the Irish a very low proportion in the highest categories. The figures which have appeared for Indians are rather surprising. Taken as they stand they suggest that 76% (as compared with the English 71%) are in the top four occupational categories and only one Indian in ten was registered as unskilled. Furthermore the Indians have a higher proportion in the professional, foremen, skilled manual, own-account and non-manual categories than any other group, although the Poles, with 71% in the top four categories, are not far behind them.

There is no way, without further field enquiry, of accounting satisfactorily for this phenomenon. It may be that Indian males, for prestige purposes, deliberately upgraded themselves occupationally on the Census schedules, although many of them are operating their own businesses, particularly in the catering trade. The Pakistanis recorded 55% in the top four categories, which is a higher proportion than the Jamaicans or Caribbeans, but much less than the Indians. It is also a higher proportion than that recorded by the Irish, a fact which again tends to discount any suggestion that skin colour is the determining factor in occupational ranking: the Cypriots also have a smaller proportion of their number in the first four occupational groups

## TABLE 33

### Occupations of Males (per cent)

| Occupational group | Eng. | Jam. | Car. | Birthplace Ind. | Pak. | Pol. | Ire. | Cyp. |
|---|---|---|---|---|---|---|---|---|
| (1) Professional | 3 | * | 1 | 14 | 10 | 7 | 2 | 1 |
| (2) Employers and managers | 9 | 1 | 1 | 10 | 11 | 13 | 3 | 10 |
| (3) Foremen, skilled manual, own account | 36 | 39 | 33 | 18 | 11 | 34 | 30 | 36 |
| (4) Non-manual | 23 | 4 | 10 | 34 | 23 | 17 | 13 | 6 |
| (5) Personal service. Semi-skilled manual, agricultural | 15 | 22 | 24 | 13 | 24 | 18 | 20 | 30 |
| (6) Unskilled manual. Armed Forces and others | 14 | 34 | 30 | 10 | 21 | 12 | 31 | 18 |
| *Number* | 3,552† | 1,389 | 1,250 | 1,097 | 211 | 1,258 | 6,143 | 883 |

Source: 10% Census analysis
* Below 0·5%.　　　　　† 1 in 25 sample.

(This table relates to a 10% sample of males aged 15 years of age and over in the 28 London metropolitan boroughs, including retired persons. The total figures differ from those in Table 32 where males under 15 are included.)

than either the Indians or the Pakistanis. In interpreting these figures it is as well to note specifically the small number of Pakistanis included in this sample. In the main Pakistani workers have settled in the north of England, for instance in Bradford, and a high proportion of the Pakistanis in London are probably full-time students excluded from these statistics.

When we examine the statistics more closely, we can discern some noticeable differences between the various boroughs of London. In the case of West Indians, for instance, the number of males classified as 'professional, employers and managers' in London as a whole was 2%, but in Kensington and Fulham the proportion was 4%. In Hammersmith 28% were classified as 'semi-skilled', but in Lewisham and Camberwell the proportion was 15%. In some boroughs the total numbers were quite small and the differences may not be statistically significant. Accordingly, in Table 34 below we exclude all boroughs which recorded seventy or less West Indian male occupied persons and condense the six occupational groups into four. The table includes the boroughs which recorded altogether 90% of the total male West Indian workers in London. These differences between the boroughs are statistically significant, although they are not easy to explain. If occupation is a measure of social class, it is possible that West Indians are beginning to disperse according to ideas of class.

TABLE 34

*Occupations of West Indian Males\* in Selected London Boroughs*

| Borough | Occupation | | | | |
|---|---|---|---|---|---|
| | Professional, employers, managers Groups 1 & 2 % | Foremen, non-manual Groups 3 & 4 % | Semi-skilled Group 5 % | Others Group 6 % | Number of male workers |
| Battersea | 2 | 36 | 24 | 39 | 109 |
| Camberwell | — | 43 | 15 | 42 | 156 |
| Fulham | 4 | 38 | 27 | 31 | 71 |
| Hackney | 1 | 50 | 20 | 30 | 278 |
| Hammersmith | 1 | 45 | 28 | 26 | 155 |
| Islington | — | 42 | 25 | 32 | 330 |
| Kensington | 4 | 46 | 26 | 24 | 211 |
| Lambeth | 1 | 37 | 24 | 39 | 392 |
| Lewisham | 2 | 39 | 15 | 43 | 94 |
| Paddington | 2 | 43 | 16 | 39 | 229 |
| Stepney | — | 33 | 26 | 41 | 78 |
| Stoke Newington | — | 61 | 24 | 15 | 74 |
| Wandsworth | 2 | 49 | 27 | 23 | 172 |
| All metropolitan boroughs | 2 | 43 | 23 | 32 | 2,633 |

*Source:* 10% Census analysis

\* 'West Indians' includes Jamaicans and Caribbeans.

(The table includes only those boroughs which recorded 70 or more West Indian males aged 15 years of age and over, excluding retired persons.)

This borough variation is no less true when we examine the experience of males born in India and Pakistan. Table 35 gives details of all boroughs in which at least forty males from those countries were enumerated in the Census. The thirteen boroughs account for 80 % of the total number of male Indians and Pakistanis living in London. The proportion recorded in the professional and managerial categories varies from 4 % in Stepney to 37 % in Hampstead whilst the overall average for the twenty-eight boroughs was 23 %. Similarly 34 % were recorded

TABLE 35

*Occupations of Male Asiatic\* Immigrants in
Selected London Boroughs*

| | Occupation | | | | |
|---|---|---|---|---|---|
| | *Professional, employers, managers* | *Foremen, non-manual* | *Semi-skilled* | *Others* | *Number of male workers* |
| *Borough* | *Groups 1 & 2* | *Groups 3 & 4* | *Group 5* | *Group 6* | |
| | % | % | % | % | |
| Fulham | 17 | 64 | 7 | 12 | 42 |
| Hackney | 8 | 51 | 25 | 16 | 51 |
| Hammersmith | 19 | 55 | 13 | 13 | 47 |
| Hampstead | 37 | 46 | 8 | 8 | 106 |
| Islington | 18 | 55 | 20 | 7 | 71 |
| Kensington | 26 | 56 | 9 | 9 | 144 |
| Lambeth | 19 | 52 | 14 | 14 | 69 |
| Lewisham | 23 | 60 | 13 | 4 | 52 |
| Paddington | 23 | 58 | 8 | 11 | 84 |
| St. Pancras | 22 | 39 | 22 | 16 | 73 |
| Stepney | 4 | 31 | 31 | 34 | 81 |
| Wandsworth | 23 | 60 | 12 | 5 | 151 |
| Woolwich | 24 | 40 | 24 | 12 | 42 |
| | | | | | |
| All metropolitan boroughs | 23 | 50 | 15 | 11 | 1,263 |

*Source:* 10% Census analysis

\* 'Asiatics' includes males born in India and Pakistan aged 15 years of age and over, excluding retired persons.

in the unskilled category in Stepney, but only 4% were so classified in Lewisham. It is probably the case that the immigrants from India and Pakistan are also dispersing themselves occupationally according to the type of district. This is only to be expected. Hampstead is a well-to-do area compared with Stepney. We need not be surprised at the distribution we observe in this respect.

We can turn from the statistics obtained from a study of the Census, and consider the information derived with regard to occupations from the Jamaican Sample Survey, which was not confined to London. The majority of the persons included in the sample of Jamaican immigrants were working either in completely unskilled or in semi-skilled occupations. Each one was asked to specify the job he or she was doing at the time of the interview, and these replies form the basis of the following analysis. There is always a danger in any enquiry in which a person is asked to state his occupation, and the reply cannot be verified either by a trial test or further enquiry at the workplace, that the person concerned will tend to exaggerate the importance of his job in order to secure additional social prestige with the interviewer. This human propensity must, therefore, be accepted as inevitable in the present enquiry although there is no reason to believe, from the nature of the replies themselves, that there was any appreciable distortion of the truth, by accident or design, in the course of the sample enquiry. Altogether 226 jobs were specified to the interviewers, and a further eight replies were given which were too vague to be classifiable. Of the 103 men who replied, 44% stated that they were engaged in an unskilled occupation, usually described as that of labourer, porter, cleaner, boilerman, stoker, factory hand, handyman or some such designation. A lower proportion (24%) of the women regarded themselves as working in unskilled jobs, as ward orderlies in hospitals, canteen assistants, domestic helps, cleaners or general labourers in factories. It seems reasonable to assume that these figures can be taken as at least the minimum so far as unskilled workers are concerned.

The next fairly clearly defined category, into which 12% of the men and 24% of the women were placed, was that including the occupations of machine operator, storekeeper or packer, occupations which require something more than sheer muscle-power and could be regarded as semi-skilled in that a certain amount of specialized training is required which varies, of course, from job to job. Machine operators were reported from the rubber, cycle, shoe and metal industries amongst the men, whereas amongst the women the textile and garment industries (for instance, raincoat manufacturing) predominated, although individuals were also employed on machines in the tobacco, radio, sugar confectionery and metal industries. Pressers in laundries were included in this category.

Semi-skilled or skilled occupations were claimed by 40% of the men and 36% of the women by giving specific names to the tasks they were performing, which appeared to require some modicum of training and experience, although there are grave difficulties inherent in any attempt to try to measure the degree of skill involved, and some of the jobs listed below may legitimately be described as 'skilled'. Amongst some of the occupations being followed were:

| Men | Women |
|---|---|
| Plastic moulder | Nurse |
| Fitter's mate | Dressmaker |
| Carpentry shuttering | Box folder |
| Plumber | Presser and folder in laundry |
| Cook | Wirer in plate factory |
| Hospital steward | Dental technician |
| Railway guard | Tailoring |
| Motor-lorry driver | Cook |
| Nurse in hospital | Chicken keeper |
| Pastry maker | Chrome polisher |
| Chemical packer | Bus conductress |
| Miner | Pie maker |
| Electrician | Cleaning photographs |
| Gardener | Bookbinding |
| Driller | |
| Bus conductor | |
| Lamp wirer | |
| Polisher of furniture | |
| Painter | |
| Optical lens maker | |
| Steel stripper | |
| Rubber shaper | |
| Medical orderly | |
| Garage mechanic | |
| Master tailor | |

Only 2% of the women—and none of the men—were engaged in office work as shorthand typists or telephone operators. A fairly large number of the women were reported to be

### TABLE 36

*Occupations of Jamaican Immigrants*
*(per cent)*

| | Male | Female |
|---|---|---|
| Unskilled | 44 | 24 |
| Machine operators, storekeepers, packers | 12 | 24 |
| Semi-skilled | 40 | 36 |
| Clerical occupations | — | 2 |
| Others | 4 | 14 |
| | 100 | 100 |
| Number of replies | 103 | 123 |
| No clear reply | 5 | 3 |

*Source:* Jamaican Sample Survey

housewives or expectant mothers. Three men and six women stated that they were unemployed, although some of the housewives would possibly take employment if they could find it (Table 36).

## Industrial Classification

The Jamaican Sample Survey also provides information about the various industries in which Jamaicans are to be found. For Jamaican males the most important industries, employing over one-third, were engineering, metal, vehicles and chemicals.[1] These industries cover a wide range of sub-categories, but men in the sample were found working in iron and steel works, sheet metal, metal tubes, mechanical engineering, screw manufacture, aircraft, motor vehicle and cycle industries, as well as manufacturing metal goods from aluminium, cutlery, and light engineering. A few of this group were employed in chemical, paint and dye factories, and in radio manufacture or repair. Transport was the next most important source of employment for men: about 5% were employed on British Railways and a few more in industries connected with road transport, including removal and warehousing. These two main groups of industries accounted for over half the employment of the males; the rest were scattered in ones and twos throughout British industry. None was engaged in agriculture (a pursuit in which many of them had been engaged in a full- or part-time capacity in Jamaica) but four of them were working in coal-mining. A few were engaged in clothing manufacture, including making leather goods and shoes; rather more in the food-processing industries (cakes, brewing, canning, potato crisps) and in furniture, cable manufacture, paper-making, optical and rubber industries. About one in ten was employed in the building and constructional industries, a few were employed in the gas industry, and about one in ten in hospitals, local government road services, and laundries. Very few were employed in catering or distribution.

The pattern of industrial employment amongst the women is completely different. Here the three most important groups of industries, accounting for two-thirds of the total employment, were hospitals, textiles and clothing, and light engineering.

[1] This broad grouping is based on that of the Standard Industrial Classification.

Almost one woman in five was employed in the hospitals, either in nursing or in domestic services: only one recorded 'domestic work', which may have been in an institution. None of the women, apparently, were working as domestic helps in private homes, a field in which their services might well have been in great demand had they themselves been willing to provide the supply. Just under one in ten was employed in laundries and almost one in five in clothing factories. One or two were engaged in textile factories, or in making socks or shoes. Those that were engaged in the engineering and metal goods industries were employed in radio assembly, manufacturing chromium ware, light electrical assembly, car components, marine accessories, cables and packing tubes. Isolated people were reported from a wide range of food-processing industries such as sweets and confectionery manufacture, ice-cream making, jellies, canned foods, pickling, brewing, soft drinks manufacture, tobacco and cattle produce. In the service industries catering was the most frequently reported (6% were engaged in this industry), only one on British Railways, 6% in road transport (probably working in depots, canteens, and so forth, not on the road) and only two in retail distribution. The manufacture of cardboard boxes and toys was mentioned once or twice, and finally one—but only one—was reported as working in an industry described as 'broilers or farming' (Table 37).

TABLE 37

*Industrial Classification of Jamaican Immigrants (per cent)*

|  | Males | Females |
|---|---|---|
| (1) Agriculture and mining | 4 | 1 |
| (2) Chemicals, metals, engineering, vehicles | 38 | 18 |
| (3) Textiles, clothing, leather | 4 | 22 |
| (4) Food manufacturing | 9 | 11 |
| (5) Wood, paper, rubber, other manufacturing | 6 | 7 |
| (6) Building | 11 | — |
| (7) Gas, electricity, water | 3 | — |
| (8) Transport, distribution | 16 | 14 |
| (9) Administration, hospitals, miscellaneous services | 9 | 27 |
|  | 100 | 100 |
| Number of persons: | 98 | 100 |

*Source:* Jamaican Sample Survey

*Methods of Obtaining Employment*

At the end of both the first and second years of the enquiry based on the Jamaican sample, the people interviewed were asked how they obtained their present (or latest) employment. By far the most important method was through the personal efforts of a relative—aunt, cousin, brother, brother-in-law, sister, wife, or husband—who was already working or had some contact in the workplace. In the first year 36% of the men and 37% of the women obtained their jobs through the personal recommendation of a relative or a friend. This proportion increased to 40% of the men and 49% of the women in the second year.

Of almost equal importance is the chance application—the 'walk and look' method as several respondents described it. Quite often the chance application is not entirely accidental—information comes through the 'grapevine' that a job might be available and the individual takes a chance by applying, without relying on any personal recommendation. In other cases the individual just walks about asking at building sites, or looking at factory notice boards. One woman reported that she had applied for a job at fifty hospitals before obtaining her employment. Altogether four jobs out of five were found either by personal recommendation or by chance application.

The public employment exchange system plays a relatively small part in the process of finding employment for migrants, if the experience recorded in this enquiry is in any way typical. Furthermore its usefulness declined sharply from the first to the second year, particularly in the case of women. In the first year almost one man in five and one woman in four obtained their jobs through the public employment exchange. In the second year, whilst the proportion of men had dropped only slightly (from 18% to 15%), the proportion of women obtaining work in this way had dropped from 26% to 7%. Cases were reported, it is true, of several jobs being obtained through the public employment exchange by the same individual. One man explained how he walked into the exchange one day, followed by an Englishman who offered him a job, and he started the following morning! Not infrequently the individuals concerned did not even try to obtain work through the exchange: in one case a woman saw an advertisement in the press, referred to it on a subsequent visit to the employment exchange and got the job with the help of the Ministry of Labour official. The Youth Employment service was mentioned only once.

Advertisements play a relatively small part in the job placement field: in the second year only one person in twenty obtained employment by following up an advertisement, usually in the local newspaper. There were two cases reported where the trade union had found a job for the individual, one in the case of a craftsman and the other a member of a general union. In one isolated instance was it reported that the services of a fee-charging private agency had been utilized (Table 38).

TABLE 38

*Securing Employment (per cent)*

| Medium | Men | | Women | |
|---|---|---|---|---|
| | *1st year* | *2nd year* | *1st year* | *2nd year* |
| Through a friend or relative | 36 | 40 | 37 | 49 |
| Chance application | 38 | 41 | 32 | 40 |
| Public employment exchange | 18 | 15 | 26 | 7 |
| Reply to advertisement | 8 | 4 | 5 | 4 |
| | 100 | 100 | 100 | 100 |
| Number of replies | 104 | 80 | 119 | 96 |
| No reply or self-employed | — | 3 | — | 10 |

*Source:* Jamaican Sample Survey

During the interviews conducted amongst the Jamaican migrants the question was asked: 'Are the conditions of employment regarded as satisfactory?' In all, there were 216 clear replies to this question (in fourteen cases the reply was ambiguous or beside the point) and they can be classified into three groups. There were those who gave an unmistakably positive reply—that the conditions of employment (as distinct from the pay, which was a source of constant complaint from probably the majority of the respondents) were satisfactory although, perhaps, a personal note of reservation was added. The second category contained the negative replies, where the conditions were clearly not regarded as satisfactory, and often quite specific complaints were made. The third group lay in between, a 'Yes, but . . .' type of reply. Analysing the replies into these groups the result was:

|                                         | *Per cent* |
| --------------------------------------- | ---------- |
| Positive—conditions satisfactory        | 57         |
| Negative—conditions unsatisfactory      | 24         |
| Yes, but . . .                          | 19         |
|                                         | 100        |

The majority of the positive replies contained no embellish-
ment; they just affirmed that the conditions were satisfactory.
Sometimes they went further, as in the case of the man who
explained that at his work they 'treat him nice' and told him
that he could stay there for the rest of his life—apparently he
plans to do just that. One man, working in a hospital, explained
how he likes night work because it is quiet and he is his own
boss, his only grumble being that he cannot prepare his own
food, Jamaican style, and has to make do with general hospital
food. This was a point made many times in the course of the
interviews: the migrants prefer to take their lunch to work and
sacrifice the subsidized canteen meals because the menu is not
to their taste. Relations with the foremen and chargehands are
of great importance and many different experiences were
reported. One man was congratulated by his foreman three
months after arrival and recommended for promotion, much to
his delight. A boss who works himself, and does not content himself with driving the workers, was the subject of favourable
comment, and a number specifically made the point that race
relations were good in the factory. One girl described how
everybody, white and coloured, was 'fun to work with'; another girl had great comfort from a particular white girl friend
in a workshop where relations between white and coloured
were good. A source of complaint, for which management cannot be blamed, concerned the English weather—the winter
causes great distress to migrants in their early years, accustomed as they are to Jamaican sunshine. The cold often causes
foot trouble. A few of the people interviewed, whilst expressing
general satisfaction at the conditions of employment, made it
clear that they personally were dissatisfied because they felt
they could do more responsible and skilled jobs than those they
were permitted to do. How far these complaints had any justi-
fication it was not possible to decide during the interviews, but
the overall picture that emerges is that over half the persons
interviewed were quite satisfied with their conditions of employment (pay scales excepted).

We can now consider the replies which have been described as 'Yes, but . . . ' Here no very clear reply is given to the direct question: 'Are the conditions of employment regarded as satisfactory?', but a catalogue of generalized complaints is given which leaves the impression of dissatisfaction without being very specific about it. The complaints are those that one would expect to receive from any group of workers selected in this fashion: they have no particular reference to the fact that the workers are immigrants. The work was sometimes described as heavy (for example, lifting heavy loads from lorries), mono- tonous, or the physical conditions were unpleasant (hot, dusty, noisy), or the worker felt that he or she was being unduly rushed (particularly when piecework was in operation). Quite a few complaints were received that the conditions of work were affecting health: that dust was affecting chest and throat or causing backache, draughts were bringing on rheumatism, or chemicals were affecting hands and chest. How far these appre- hensions had any basis in reality could not be ascertained: they were, however, very real fears in the minds of the persons giving expression to them. A minority were discontented because they felt the job held no prospects for them and they would like to improve themselves. Long distances from home to work were also mentioned several times. The canteen was mentioned by several respondents and complaints made about the food or drink served in it.

It is worthy of note that, out of the 216 replies, only five made specific reference to any alleged colour discrimination at work. One woman alleged that the firm employing her is racially prejudiced because every time a coloured person leaves a white worker is taken on in her place, and coloured applicants for jobs are turned away when there are vacancies. The same woman explained that she personally is given respon- sibility to supervise several other coloured girls when the fore- woman is absent. One man alleged that whilst the 'boss' likes coloured workers, the foreman does not, and always gives them the worst work—most of the day shift are white whilst most of the night shift are coloured. Another man said that the union steward is also the foreman and so complaints are impossible in a place where coloured people are 'pushed around and bossed around'. Whites get an afternoon tea-break, but not coloureds. At the end of the week whites are allowed off work half an hour early, but not coloureds. If a coloured man stays off work one day he is not allowed to work the following day. One man claimed that 'coloured people are treated like animals': another said that overtime is given only to white workers, not to coloured. He went on to explain that even if he could work overtime he did not think he would, as he would have more taken off him in income tax.

These specific complaints regarding alleged racial discrimination have been included here not because they have any great significance in the sample as a whole but simply to illustrate the sort of comments that were made by that tiny minority of the migrants who gave expression to any kind of sentiment that they were experiencing racial discrimination at work. It was suggested at the beginning of this chapter that race relations in industry could become a most explosive subject if ever full employment disappeared and unemployment returned with white workers competing for jobs which coloured workers hold at present. This is certainly a real danger, but there was no evidence in the present enquiry to suggest that it is in any way a major problem at present. Quite the reverse: there is ample evidence from the 216 replies received during this investigation that racial frictions in British industry are minimal, and such tensions as do arise occur in no greater or lesser degree than they would amongst a heterogeneous group of workers anywhere.

# Chapter V

## UNEMPLOYMENT

THE problem of unemployment amongst immigrant workers constantly exercises the minds of officials and those members of the public who interest themselves in the question of Britain's immigration policies. Fears are constantly expressed that an increase in immigration will lead to an increased incidence of unemployment amongst the immigrants, who would thereby become a public liability. It is widely believed that even a minor economic recession in Britain would lead to an increase in unemployment of greater severity amongst immigrant groups than the native population. The contrary fear is also sometimes expressed, that if a rise in unemployment generally resulted in a rise of unemployment amongst the native population, but not amongst the immigrants, an increase in racial tension might be expected. It may, therefore, be worth while to examine the statistics at present available which cast some light on this matter, in so far as past experience is any guide.

TABLE 39

### Total Registered Unemployed in Great Britain, August 1960 to May 1962

| Period | Total (000) | Rate % | Males (000) | Females (000) |
|---|---|---|---|---|
| August 1960 | 322 | 1·4 | 230 | 92 |
| November 1960 | 352 | 1·6 | 255 | 97 |
| February 1961 | 390 | 1·7 | 286 | 104 |
| May 1961 | 300 | 1·3 | 215 | 85 |
| August 1961 | 305 | 1·4 | 221 | 84 |
| November 1961 | 388 | 1·7 | 287 | 101 |
| February 1962 | 454 | 2·0 | 337 | 117 |
| May 1962 | 424 | 1·9 | 311 | 113 |

*Source:* Ministry of Labour

(The 'rate %' is the number registered as unemployed expressed as a percentage of the estimated total number of employees.)

Before examining the incidence and characteristics of unemployment amongst coloured workers, it is as well to recapitu-
late the unemployment situation in the country as a whole, in
the period August 1960 to May 1962. The number of unemployed varies seasonally and although there was a slight rise in
the unemployment rate this was not serious. In May 1962, the
unemployment rate was 1·9%, that is, 0·6% higher than in May
1961. Similarly the figure in February 1962 of 2·0% was 0·3%
higher than that of the same period the previous year (Table
39).

TABLE 40

*Unemployed Coloured Immigrants from Commonwealth Territories
registered for Employment at Local Offices of the Ministry of Labour,
August 1960 to May 1962*

| | | Coloured males | | Coloured females | |
| | Total | | Total % | | Total % |
| | coloured | Number | of male | Number | of female |
| Date | unemployed | unemployed | unemployed | unemployed | unemployed |
|---|---|---|---|---|---|
| 2 August 1960 | 8,355 | 5,557 | 2·4 | 2,798 | 3·0 |
| 1 November 1960 | 11,712 | 7,441 | 2·9 | 4,271 | 4·4 |
| 7 February 1961 | 14,281 | 9,126 | 3·2 | 5,155 | 5·0 |
| 2 May 1961 | 15,082 | 9,093 | 4·2 | 5,989 | 7·0 |
| 1 August 1961 | 13,926 | 8,623 | 3·9 | 5,303 | 6·3 |
| 7 November 1961 | 21,712 | 14,130 | 4·9 | 7,582 | 7·5 |
| 6 February 1962 | 31,683 | 22,516 | 6·7 | 9,167 | 7·8 |
| 1 May 1962 | 38,569 | 27,793 | 8·9 | 10,776 | 9·5 |

*Source:* Ministry of Labour

(The figures include those registered as 'temporarily stopped'. They include both
claimants and non-claimants of unemployment benefit.)

Once a quarter, prior to July 1962, each local employment
exchange of the United Kingdom Ministry of Labour made a
count of the coloured unemployed workers (both claimants and
non-claimants for insurance) registered on their books, and
made a report to headquarters if the number exceeded 100, and
these figures are given in Table 40 above. With the aid of this
table we can consider the experience of unemployment amongst
the coloured population. We must begin by observing that in
absolute numbers the coloured unemployed rose sharply from
around 8,000 in August 1960 to around 38,000 in May 1962,
the really serious increase occurring after November 1961

(when there were some 21,000 coloured unemployed). This sharp rise after November 1961 coincided with the passing through Parliament of the new restrictive legislation on immigration which was forecast in a speech by the then Home Secretary at a Conservative Party Conference in November 1961. The rising crescendo of migration to Britain immediately after that date from countries like Jamaica was undoubtedly related to these political events, and in the last days of June 1962, just before the Act came into force, the Press was full of pictures and stories of West Indians and other Commonwealth citizens chartering planes to 'beat the ban'. This artificial stimulation to the inflow of labour caused difficulties of immediate absorption which resulted in a rise in the number of coloured unemployed people.

Even so, it remains clear that the coloured unemployment rate was higher in the period prior to June 1962 than that recorded amongst the indigenous population. Furthermore as the immigrants tend to crowd into areas where the indigenous unemployment rate tends to be below the national average, the situation is even more severe than a study of the national averages might imply. But how high was the rate of coloured unemployment? This cannot be known because there are no accurate figures of the number of coloured people at work. (The M.P.N.I. statistics of entrants to the labour force are not useful for this purpose.) But some indication of the size of the problem is available from a comparison of the proportion of coloured unemployed to the total unemployed. This rose sharply particularly in the last two years before the new Act came into force. The coloured unemployed were 2·4% of the total unemployed in August 1960, and the proportion rose more or less steadily until May 1962. It reached 3·9% in August 1961, then rose in November 1961, again in February 1962, and again to an all-time high of 8·9% in May 1962. By that month just under one unemployed person in eleven in Britain was coloured; the proportion was very much worse in areas of concentration of coloured people. The position as regards women has followed the same trend as that of men, but with a more rapid rise. By May 1962, 9·5% of unemployed females were coloured.

The coloured unemployed were not uniformly distributed throughout the country. There was marked concentration in particular regions and, although this cannot be proved from the official statistics, they also tended to concentrate within regions; within the London area, for instance, the Brixton and the Willesden exchanges had a marked preponderance of coloured unemployed. This is only to be expected from the residential concentrations of coloured people in particular districts of the main cities (Brixton, Willesden, Stoke Newington in London, Handsworth in Birmingham, Moss Side in Manchester). The residential concentration (and, consequently, the unemployment concentration) is more marked than the workplace concentration. Coloured workers are found working in all parts of London (for example, on the transport system) and it is quite common for factories in the suburban outer belt to send buses into Brixton in the morning, collect a coloured labour force and return them to Brixton at night. Almost half the coloured unemployed (43%) were to be found in London. Just over a quarter (29%) were in the Midlands, 14% in Yorkshire and Lincolnshire and 7% in the north-west.

## Unemployment after 1962

The Commonwealth Immigrants Act came into force in July 1962 and in the following year, in February 1963, the Ministry of Labour changed the basis of counting the unemployed from the Commonwealth. The count is now taken quarterly, as before, in August, November, February and May on the first Monday in the month, but instead of reporting on the 'coloured' unemployed, the managers of the local employment exchanges included in the enquiry record the unemployed in territories grouped as follows:

(a) Australia, Canada and New Zealand
(b) Cyprus, Gibraltar and Malta
(c) Africa
(d) West Indies
(e) India
(f) Pakistan
(g) Others

It follows, therefore, that the statistics derived from this new basis are not exactly comparable with those of the 'coloured' unemployed prepared prior to July 1962 but it is not unreasonable to assume that groups (c) to (g) inclusive consist predominantly of 'coloured' persons.[1]

In the period from August 1962 to November 1964, the total number of registered unemployed varied very little, apart from an unusual upsurge in February 1963. The number of unemployed males varied between 270,000 and 413,000 and in employed females between 91,000 and 141,000 (excluding February 1963). The national percentage of unemployment remained fairly constant at less than 2·5% apart from the exceptionally high rate of 3·9% in February 1963. Indeed, the trend was downward.

Against this national background we can set the recorded experience of unemployed persons from the Commonwealth. This too showed a downward trend for both males and females. In August 1962 almost 7% of the male and 7·5% of the female unemployed were born in the Commonwealth. Since then the proportions have dropped almost steadily, quarter by quarter, until by November 1964 the proportions were 2·0% of the males and 3·4% of the females (Table 41).

TABLE 41

*Registered Unemployed in Great Britain,\**
*August 1962 to November 1964*

(a) MALES

| Month | Total registered unemployed (thousands) | Commonwealth unemployed (thousands) | National % of unemployment (male and female)† | Commonwealth unemployed percentage‡ |
|---|---|---|---|---|
| August 1962 | 340·2 | 23·6 | 2·1 | 6·9 |
| November 1962 | 409·5 | 21·0 | 2·4 | 5·1 |
| February 1963 | 721·9 | 28·1 | 3·9 | 3·9 |
| May 1963 | 412·5 | 18·1 | 2·4 | 4·4 |
| August 1963 | 369·0 | 13·4 | 2·2 | 3·6 |
| November 1963 | 353·4 | 12·3 | 2·1 | 3·5 |
| February 1964 | 350·3 | 12·6 | 2·0 | 3·6 |
| May 1964 | 277·9 | 7·5 | 1·6 | 2·7 |
| August 1964 | 272·0 | 6·0 | 1·6 | 2·2 |
| November 1964 | 260·9 | 5·1 | 1·5 | 2·0 |

[1] The Ministry of Labour has again been good enough to permit the unpublished figures to be used in the present study. Now that the revised basis of counting has removed even the slightest suggestion of 'colour discrimination' there does not appear to be any valid reason why the figures as prepared, being in the public interest, should not be published regularly in the Ministry of Labour *Gazette*.

TABLE 41 *(cont.)*

(b) FEMALES

| August 1962 | 124·2 | 9·3 | — | 7·5 |
| November 1962 | 135·2 | 8·7 | — | 6·4 |
| February 1963 | 156·4 | 8·6 | — | 5·5 |
| May 1963 | 141·1 | 8·3 | — | 5·9 |
| August 1963 | 133·0 | 5·6 | — | 4·2 |
| November 1963 | 121·0 | 4·8 | — | 4·0 |
| February 1964 | 113·8 | 4·7 | — | 4·1 |
| May 1964 | 91·2 | 3·6 | — | 3·9 |
| August 1964 | 96·5 | 3·0 | — | 3·1 |
| November 1964 | 88·9 | 3·0 | — | 3·4 |

*Source:* Ministry of Labour

\* The count of Commonwealth citizens unemployed does not include boys and girls under 18 years of age, but the national unemployment figure does. Ideally, a comparison should be made between Commonwealth unemployed and adult unemployed.

† The number of males and females registered as unemployed expressed as a percentage of the estimated total number of employees.

‡ Unemployed persons from the Commonwealth expressed as a percentage of the national unemployed.

As might be expected, there are variations in the experiences of the immigrants from different parts of the Commonwealth. Broadly speaking, as Table 42 shows, the 'coloured' immigrants form the majority of the Commonwealth unemployed— especially those from the West Indies and Pakistan. But this

TABLE 42

*Commonwealth Unemployed by Territory of Origin*
*August 1962 to November 1964*

|  | Territory of Origin (a) MALES | | | | | | Per cent | | Number all |
| Month | Aust., Can., N.Z. | Cyp., Gib., Malta | Africa | West Indies | India | Pakis- tan | Others | Total | Common- wealth |
|---|---|---|---|---|---|---|---|---|---|
| Aug. 1962 | 1 | 2 | 7 | 33 | 12 | 41 | 4 | 100 | 23,584 |
| Nov. 1962 | 1 | 3 | 8 | 36 | 12 | 36 | 4 | 100 | 21,044 |
| Feb. 1963 | 1 | 4 | 8 | 46 | 11 | 27 | 3 | 100 | 28,077 |
| May 1963 | 1 | 4 | 9 | 41 | 12 | 29 | 4 | 100 | 18,107 |
| Aug. 1963 | 1 | 4 | 10 | 32 | 18 | 31 | 4 | 100 | 13,380 |
| Nov. 1963 | 1 | 5 | 10 | 25 | 17 | 38 | 4 | 100 | 12,257 |
| Feb. 1964 | 1 | 5 | 10 | 26 | 12 | 42 | 4 | 100 | 12,550 |
| May 1964 | 2 | 7 | 15 | 32 | 12 | 28 | 5 | 100 | 7,469 |
| Aug. 1964 | 1 | 7 | 13 | 35 | 12 | 26 | 6 | 100 | 5,994 |
| Nov. 1964 | 2 | 7 | 15 | 37 | 13 | 21 | 5 | 100 | 5,084 |

TABLE 42 *(cont)*.

| | | | (b) FEMALES | | | | | | |
|---|---|---|---|---|---|---|---|---|---|
| Aug. 1962 | I | I | 6 | 88 | 2 | I | I | 100 | 9,273 |
| Nov. 1962 | I | I | 7 | 88 | 2 | * | I | 100 | 8,681 |
| Feb. 1963 | I | I | 6 | 89 | 2 | * | I | 100 | 8,597 |
| May 1963 | * | I | 6 | 89 | 2 | * | I | 100 | 8,290 |
| Aug. 1963 | I | I | 9 | 84 | 3 | I | 2 | 100 | 5,636 |
| Nov. 1963 | I | I | 12 | 82 | 3 | I | I | 100 | 4,818 |
| Feb. 1964 | I | I | 11 | 83 | 3 | * | I | 100 | 4,702 |
| May 1964 | I | I | 10 | 82 | 3 | I | 2 | 100 | 3,589 |
| Aug. 1964 | I | I | 15 | 77 | 4 | I | 2 | 100 | 3,017 |
| Nov. 1964 | I | I | 15 | 76 | 4 | I | 2 | 100 | 3,039 |

*Source:* Ministry of Labour

* Less than 0·5%.

(The count of Commonwealth unemployment is taken on the first Monday of each month.)

may be no more than a reflection of their numerical preponderance in the Commonwealth immigrant groups. Since we do not know how many of the various groups are in the labour force, we have no way of knowing whether the unemployment rate is higher among, for example, Australians than among Jamaicans.

## Unemployment in 1961

During the 1961 Census, every tenth household, it will be recalled, completed a full Census schedule. For our analysis, the computer identified persons born in Jamaica, the rest of the British West Indies ('Caribbeans'), India, Pakistan, Poland, Ireland and Cyprus who were found amongst this 10% sample and analysed them separately. In the case of persons born in England a one-in-twenty-five sample was also selected. In the full Census schedule the respondents who were in employment were asked to answer a number of questions concerning their employer's business, occupation, place of work, hours worked, and whether they worked full- or part-time. In the case of persons who were out of employment, they were either defined as 'housewife', 'student', and so forth, or were required to give details of their last employer and last occupation. It was thus possible to define the number of 'economically active persons', or workers, so as to exclude all persons under the age of fifteen years, retired persons, housewives, students, and others. A special column in the Census schedule was to be completed if the person was out of employment, although otherwise economically active (that is, was unemployed).

These figures were obtained for each birthplace group in each of the twenty-eight metropolitan boroughs. They have been aggregated in Table 43, which shows the percentage of unemployed as a percentage of the economically active population for each of the separate birthplace groups.

This table demonstrates clearly that the incidence of unemployment in London in April 1961 differed according to the birthplace category, the differences being more noticeable in the case of males than females. The unemployment rate, at 3·2%, was lowest amongst males born in England and highest, at 7·4%, amongst males born in Jamaica. Males from the rest of the Caribbean area recorded 6·0%, lower than the Jamaicans

TABLE 43

*Unemployment amongst Selected Birthplace Groups in London, April 1961*

| (a) MALES | | |
|---|---|---|
| Birthplace | % Unemployed | No. of workers* |
| England | 3·2 | 3,236† |
| Jamaica | 7·4 | 1,387 |
| Caribbean | 6·0 | 1,246 |
| India | 4·4 | 1,058 |
| Pakistan | 5·4 | 205 |
| Poland | 4·2 | 1,131 |
| Ireland | 4·8 | 5,977 |
| Cyprus | 5·8 | 869 |
| (b) FEMALES | | |
| England | 2·5 | 2,138† |
| Jamaica | 6·8 | 884 |
| Caribbean | 7·6 | 687 |
| India | 3·7 | 541 |
| Pakistan | — | 28 |
| Poland | 6·3 | 316 |
| Ireland | 2·6 | 3,986 |
| Cyprus | 2·5 | 354 |

*Source:* 10% Census analysis

* These are economically active persons whether in employment or out of employment. Persons under 15 years of age, housewives, students, etc., are excluded. Retired persons are also excluded.

† 1 in 25 sample.

but higher than the Cypriots (5·8%), and the Irish (4·8%). The number of Pakistanis was so few that the figure in their case is probably of little significance, and there was a relatively low rate (4·4%) amongst Indian males. The Polish males recorded 4·2%, which is not much higher than the English.

In all birthplace categories, apart from the Caribbean and Poland, the incidence of female unemployment was lower than amongst the males. Amongst females those born in the Caribbean (7·6% unemployed) were in the least favourable position, as compared with Jamaicans (6·8%) and Poles (6·3%). We can once more discount the Pakistanis, as the numbers are insignificant, and note again the relatively low rate (3·7%) recorded by the Indians. Females born in Ireland and Cyprus seem to have less difficulty in obtaining employment than their menfolk, and amongst the English females, who recorded 2·5% unemployment, the problem seems to be minimal. Of course a woman out of work may well have described herself as a 'housewife', and therefore be excluded from the figures and yet she might again take employment were it available to her.

These statistics are not easy to interpret. In recent years, coloured immigrants appear to have a higher unemployment rate than do other groups. This fact might be interpreted as a reflection of discrimination in employment; but it might reflect the kind of jobs that coloured immigrants occupy. It might merely refer to only one part of the immigrant population— perhaps newly arrived unskilled workers account for most of the unemployment. From Census figures alone we cannot say.

## Chapter VI

## HOUSEHOLD BUDGETS

A SERIOUS and consistent effort was made during the two-year period to try to assess the economic position of the Jamaican households included in the random sample by means of a detailed enquiry into their income and expenditure. The nature of the enquiry was defined at the outset: it was to attempt to construct an average weekly household budget for the household of which the individual in the sample formed part, the household being defined as a group of persons living under the same roof and eating communally. Because of the wide variety of relationships which are known to exist between men, women and children in Jamaican households, it was not always possible to conduct the analysis in terms of the conventional family unit, consisting of man, wife and children as the normal pattern. Although the definition of the household unit adopted was clearly stated, one of the first difficulties which faced the interviewer was to apply this definition in particular cases. It was sometimes found, for example, that a girl working and occupying one room would have a 'boy friend' who regularly visited her and in part supported her, often being the father of her children or expected baby. In other cases a large and rather amorphous group of adults, perhaps, but not always, related in some way, lived in a fairly loose kind of community in a large house, sleeping in separate rooms but sharing certain services in common (such as a common electric iron or television set). In cases like these the only practical thing to do was to try to assess the income of the household as a whole and then to correlate the expenditure of the same group of people with the income of the groups as a whole. This immediately led to the problem of securing an accurate reply to intensely personal questions about finance. Now and again, but surprisingly seldom, the interviewer encountered a hostile family which answered questions reluctantly and refused to discuss their finances at all. There were far more cases where the people questioned were not only perfectly willing to give the information requested but went to the trouble of producing pay slips to prove their stated incomes. In some cases the interviewer was able to check at the place of employment (without disclosing the identity of the individual) that the answers given were reasonably accurate. It was not always easy, of course, to get an 'average' figure—the rigorous methods customary in budget surveys could not be applied in this situation because of the relatively unsophisticated nature of many of the households, not used to social and economic surveys and more than a little suspicious of the motives of the interviewer, at least initially. For this reason a rigid insistence upon information relating to a particular pay week, for example, would simply not have been practical. Where possible the pay slip for the week preceding the enquiry was examined, and an attempt then made to decide whether this was reasonably typical, given fluctuations in income because of variations in overtime, bonuses, shift work, short time and—in at least two cases—the incidence of short-term strikes.

It was quite common experience to find that although the persons being interviewed were perfectly willing to disclose their personal income, they were vague about the incomes of other members of the household. A woman would quite often say that she had no knowledge of the income of her husband or her partner. Brothers frequently do not reveal to their sisters the amount of their earnings, far less to their brothers-in-law. Some people obtained part-time earnings or income in kind, but it was not always possible to get any idea of the amount. It was obvious, too, that sometimes the information given was wrong —it was difficult to reconcile a stated small wage with the standard of furnishing. Sometimes the demeanour of the person interviewed suggested that the answer was not truthful. Sometimes a statement made in one part of the interview would be inadvertently contradicted later in another part. These difficulties and hazards have to be overcome in any enquiry of this kind and it is not suggested that they were excessive in this one. The refusals and hesitations were not surprising: it was, on the contrary, most remarkable that many of those interviewed readily gave detailed information about their personal affairs. Indeed, it is encouraging to know this, and future surveys might well produce further details about this admittedly difficult subject.

The main difficulty encountered in this expenditure analysis was not that people would not give the information but that in quite a large number of cases they simply *could* not do so. The aim was to get an overall picture of *household* income and expenditure but the complicated structure of some of the households made this an extremely difficult task in many cases: so often there was an inextricable mixture of communal and individual spending and a high degree of genuine ignorance between the parties. For example one man shared a room with his brother, but as they worked shifts they did not cater together—they often had meals at different times, and neither knew what the other spent. Sometimes a sister would pay the rent and a brother would pay for food: neither party attempted any book-keeping in connection with this arrangement.

TABLE 44

*Average Income*

|  | End of first year | End of second year | % increase or decrease |
|---|---|---|---|
| Men | £10. 15s. od. | £11. 8s. 7d. | +6 |
| Women | £6. 13s. od. | £6. 10s. od. | −2 |

*Source:* Jamaican Sample Survey

The interviewers were asked to record the income of the household showing separately the incomes of men and of women. The average position which was revealed in the sample as a whole is contained in Table 44. It is interesting to compare these figures with the national average of earnings at approximately the same period of time. The Ministry of Labour conducts a periodical survey into earnings in Britain as a whole, and, according to the official statistics thus produced, average earnings for manual workers in Britain in October 1962 were:

| Men | £15. 17s. 3d. |
|---|---|
| Women | £8. os. 10d. |

If the figures from the sample survey can be taken as any guide to the average earnings of the Jamaican immigrants as a whole, this suggests that Jamaican men in 1962 were earning £11. 8s. 7d. per week, some 30% less than the average, and women on average were earning £6. 10s. od. per week, or some 20% less than the average. There is nothing inherently unreasonable in these figures—the migrants tend to find their way into the lower-paid jobs in the lower-paid industries.

At the end of the first year 44% of the households had a recorded average weekly income of under £10: by the end of the second year this proportion had fallen to 36%, with corresponding adjustments in the higher income brackets. These figures could be interpreted in many ways—reflecting the general rise in incomes, a greater productivity, decrease in unemployment, or move to higher-paid jobs as length of stay extends. The facts revealed by the sample survey are reproduced in Table 45.

TABLE 45

*Weekly Jamaican Household Income (per cent of households)*

| Household weekly income | First year | Second year |
| --- | --- | --- |
| Under £5 | 5 | 2 |
| £5 under £10 | 39 | 34 |
| £10 under £15 | 24 | 27 |
| £15 under £20 | 25 | 24 |
| £20 and over | 7 | 13 |
| | 100 | 100 |
| Number of households in sample | 177 | 95 |

*Source:* Jamaican Sample Survey

It was just as difficult to get information about expenditure. In a small minority of cases—less than 10%—the attempt to obtain information under this heading failed not because the person being interviewed declined to co-operate, but because some other person in the household was hostile to the project. For example, a mother refused to allow her son to answer the questions; in another interview, the girl being interviewed was planning a big wedding for herself and the interviewer believed that she resisted questions about her finances as the husband-to-be was outside the door, objecting!

On the other hand, the survey sometimes produced budgets of surprising exactitude. One household expenditure report was very explicit:

5s. each person at a time every one or two weeks for gas;
8s. approx. per week in winter for oil;
£4 for husband and self weekly for food;
5s. per week for wife and 8s. husband for clothing and footwear;
Husband £1, wife 9s. for transport;

Husband to mother 30s. and wife 15s. per week;

The joint balance of approx. £3. 15s. is disposed of as follows: joint savings, clothes, amusement, smoking by husband and very occasional drink by both in local pub. Do not bet or play bingo or do the pools.

Between these extremes of complete vagueness and remarkable precision were many reports of varying reliability; very few, however, were patently ridiculous, although not infrequently the interviewer had to give up in despair in the face of vague replies from people who claimed to have 'no idea' how they had spent their money.

One item of expenditure which was given clearly and usually without hesitation was rent—even where no other useful information could be obtained. Unfortunately the figures are not easy to interpret, for not infrequently the 'rent' included payment for services apart from house room—electricity, gas, oil, furniture hire and use of communal services such as kitchen utensils was often, in fact probably in most cases, included in the rent. Miss E., for instance, pays a rent which includes gas and baths—the landlord provides an oil heater, but not the oil, of which Miss E. has a five-gallon tank in her room (cost 12s. 6d.) which lasts for just under two weeks. (Rent books, incidentally, were often not available.)

It was also usually possible to get a reasonable estimate of the weekly amount spent on food, although this was not as definite as the rent. From what we were told, it was clear that like most immigrants in any country, Jamaicans at first have a great nostalgia for familiar diets—yams, saltfish and ackee, sweet potatoes. The latter cost 1s. 9d. for four, and one family paid 4s. a tin for ackee. Jamaican food is now available in many centres of England (Brixton Market in some respects is beginning to resemble Coronation Market in Kingston, Jamaica, in the food stalls) but the prices are still relatively high. They are certainly very much higher than they are in Jamaica, where bananas are expensive if they cost one penny each—assuming they cannot be cut down from a tree in the yard or country plot.

An item of expenditure which occurred frequently was periodic remittance to Jamaica. This payment is usually unsystematic—it is a residual and our investigators were frequently told that cash and gifts were sent to Jamaica at irregular intervals wherever they could be afforded or when there had been a chance to save some money. Very often funds were accumulated until a reasonable sum (say £5 or more) was available, then it would be remitted. It was not easy to find out the amount which had been sent in the period since the arrival of the informant in Britain, but figures between £100 and £150 were mentioned. Usually the money is accumulated by saving small items week by week, but this is not an invariable practice —occasionally the 'pardner' jackpot is used and occasionally the money is borrowed. In the main, the money seems to be sent to assist in the maintenance of children in Jamaica and is then sent to the mother, grandmother, relative or friend who has the care of the children, but this is not invariably the case. One man said he sent money to his elder brother 'because my brother looked after me when my parents died', and one woman sent money back to her sister. Other reasons given were: to save in a building society in Jamaica to buy a house; to repay a loan from family or lawyer, or lent to pay the fare to England; and one man apparently still attempts to send a tithe of his income to support his church in Jamaica. The remittances are usually sent in cash, but not always. Not infrequently we were told that parcels of clothing were sent and money was also sent to travel agents to buy air passages for children to come to Britain. Not a single individual reported that money had been sent to invest in Jamaica Government bonds or other investments in Jamaica, except for the occasional deposit to buy a house.

The amount spent on clothes was again very difficult to assess, as the expenditure is erratic and no clear records are kept. Individuals varied widely, from the people who said they had bought hardly any clothes or had to rely on second-hand ones, to those who spent 'plenty' and had cultivated a taste for hand-tailored suits at twenty-three guineas each. Clearly much depends on the stock of clothes brought into England and whether the individual arrived in summer or winter. The initial expenditure on clothes seems to have come as a considerable surprise to many people and when pressed to try to estimate realistically how much they had spent in this direction, they expressed astonishment at the size of the total. In only one or two cases was it reported that clothes were bought on hire purchase or through a clothing club—the 'pardner' jackpot was occasionally mentioned as a source of supply of funds to meet large occasional expenditure on clothing and footwear. In most cases the income is so low and the expenditure on necessities is so high that people have little left over for the luxuries of life—the family in which no one smoked or drank, rarely went out or bought clothes was by no means untypical. Weddings and babies are heavy items of expenditure when they arise and may take years of self-dcnial to finance. Very little appears to be spent on basic furnishings such as linoleum or curtains, which are usually provided by the landlord— although occasionally an expensive radiogram appeared in the budget. One or two confessed that they occasionally bought rum to keep the cold out or keep their spirits up; each member of one family apparently drinks a bottle of stout per day. In only one or two cases was drink anything of a problem—one

## TABLE 46

### *Analysis of Expenditure of Jamaican Households*

*Expenditure as % of total income*

(a) FIRST YEAR

*London Area*

| Income group (£ per week) | Rent | Food | To Jamaica |
|---|---|---|---|
| 5 under 10 | 28 | 33 | 9 |
| 10 under 15 | 20 | 26 | 13 |
| 15 under 20 | 16 | 26 | 11 |
| 20 and over* | 16 | 21 | 8 |

*Provinces*

| | Rent | Food | To Jamaica |
|---|---|---|---|
| 5 under 10 | 26 | 35 | 13 |
| 10 under 15 | 20 | 30 | 13 |
| 15 under 20 | 15 | 29 | 15 |
| 20 and over | — | — | — |

(b) SECOND YEAR

*London and Provinces*

| | Rent | Food | To Jamaica |
|---|---|---|---|
| 5 under 10 | 27 | 34 | 11 |
| 10 under 15 | 19 | 34 | 16 |
| 15 under 20 | 14 | 21 | 9 |
| 20 and over† | 12 | 24 | 11 |

*Source:* Jamaican Sample Survey

* 3 had household incomes of £20–£21 weekly, 1 had an income of over £21 but had under £22, 4 had £22–£24, 2 had £25–£26, 2 had £26–£27.

† 5 had household incomes of £20–£21 per week, 2 had over £21 and under £22 per week, 1 had £24 and 1 had £27.

man living alone said he drank heavily and took occasional
nips during the interview to fortify himself against further
questioning, but only one husband was reported by the wife
to go on solo drinking sprees on Saturday nights. Only one item,
too, of an educational nature was clearly specified: one girl
had bought a Salvation Army hat and was saving up to buy the
full uniform. She had also bought three leather-bound 'general
knowledge' books for £6. Taking all the budgets together the
average position in so far as it can be estimated is recorded in
Table 46, which analyses average expenditure by a series of
income groups.

The figures follow a reasonable pattern—rents in London are
only slightly higher as a percentage of income as compared
with the provinces, for although the absolute level of rents is
higher, the average income also is higher. In the lowest income
bracket of all, rent takes over a quarter of the total income, but
the proportion spent on rent falls progressively as income rises
to £15 a week, when it appears to level off. Food expenditure
shows a similar trend, falling progressively through the income
ranges. The amount sent to Jamaica is decidedly erratic and no
very clear generalization can be made, except to say that there
is no evidence of a correlation between the size of the income
and the remittance to Jamaica: it is a far from constant figure
but seems to vary between 10% to 15% of the total: people
living in the provinces tend to send rather more than people in
London, but the evidence on this point is far from conclusive.
There is no sign, as yet, of any substantial falling-off of remittances to Jamaica, comparing the first year with the second
(the unweighted average over all income groups in the first
year was 11·7% and in the second year 11·3%) but it would be
premature to assume that migrants to England, once they have
established themselves, will continue to remit a relatively high
proportion of their income to Jamaica indefinitely.

Expenditure on rent, food and remittances to Jamaica leaves
no visible trace behind, but money spent on household durable
goods can be seen in the accumulation of furnishings and property. As a separate method of estimating the material welfare
of the persons included in the study as it changed over the two-
year period, and as an indication of their order of preferences
in the scale of expenditure on household belongings in each of
the years, each household was asked to state whether or not it

owned a given item of equipment. In most cases the response to this question was immediate and unhesitating; in any event the interviewer could see whether or not a given item was visible in or around the house where the interview took place. The question specifically asked whether the respondent had bought or was hiring the equipment for his or her own use. In quite a number of cases tenants appear to have the use of some of these things (for instance, electric iron, radio, television set) as part of the communal services provided by the landlord which are charged for in the rent. The results are given in Table 47, in which there is clear evidence of increasing prosperity. The proportion possessing electric irons, radios, record players and television sets increased quite substantially from the date of arrival to the end of the second year. Refrigerators, washing machines and cocktail cabinets are not part of the standard pattern of life nor have the migrants, as yet, joined the great motoring public. Less than 5 %, even at the end of the second year, claimed to have a car, motor-cycle, scooter, or garage.

TABLE 47

*Household Possessions (per cent of sample)*

| Item possessed | End of first year | End of second year |
|---|---|---|
| Electric iron | 52 | 68 |
| Radio | 47 | 66 |
| Record player or tape recorder | 32 | 46 |
| Television set | 22 | 35 |
| Cocktail cabinet | 4 | 5 |
| Car | | |
| Motor-cycle or scooter | | |
| Garage | Less than 5% | |
| Refrigerator | | |
| Washing machine | | |
| None of the above | | 13 |

*Source:* Jamaican Sample Survey

One of the most unpleasant surprises which Jamaican migrants experience once they start to work in England is the amount of money deducted at source from their income under the P.A.Y.E. system. Very few of them have had any direct experience of this system in Jamaica, where a P.A.Y.E. scheme operates but usually begins to take effect only for incomes higher than those that most of the migrants had attained in their homeland. Time and again during the enquiry people complained of the high level of income taxation. Part of the distress is due to the unfamiliarity of the concept of direct personal taxation, although a minority of the sample interviewed have accepted it with, at least, resignation as 'the English way of life' and not so painful because it is deducted at source.

There were also a large number of cases where there appears to be quite genuine hardship and overpayment of tax. Where the household conformed to the traditional English pattern of husband, legally married wife and children resident with them there appeared to be little difficulty. The problems arose from ignorance on the part of the claimants, an unco-operative tax office, problems of proving claims and, in some cases, simple inertia born of a feeling of hopelessness which in turn derived from the experiences of friends and neighbours. At the end of the first year, enquiries established that 78% of the sample were paying income tax (80% of the men and 76% of the women), of whom just over one-third (35%) said they were obtaining tax reliefs for children they were supporting in Jamaica. Of those who said they were not obtaining such reliefs just over half (55%) said they had tried to obtain them, and 45% said they had made no effort.

At the end of the second year the position was investigated again and the results are embodied in Table 48.

TABLE 48

*Income Tax Reliefs at End of Second Year*
*(per cent of sample)*

|  |  |
|---|---|
| Applied for relief of income tax for children being supported in Jamaica | 48 |
| *Not* applied for such reliefs (including non-tax payers) | 44 |
| No reply | 8 |
|  | 100 |
| *Of those applying for such relief:* |  |
| Relief obtained | 58 |
| Not obtained | 42 |
|  | 100 |

*Source:* Jamaican Sample Survey

A fairly high proportion of those who had not obtained relief where they appeared to be entitled to it, had either not bothered to apply, or were ignorant of the existence of such reliefs and how to set about obtaining them. Many of those knowing of the possibility of reliefs but making no effort to obtain them explained that they 'could not be bothered' to fill in so many forms or spend hours arguing at the tax office (losing pay in the process) when they were convinced, from the experience of their friends, that their applications would be refused in the end.

The biggest single problem identified was the difficulty of getting adequate documentary proof from Jamaica that they were in fact supporting the children on whose account they claimed tax relief. Birth certificates and marriage certificates are not easy to obtain in Jamaica and although the tax offices will usually accept a letter in evidence from a Justice of the Peace, even this is not always easy to arrange. Tales were told of grandmothers too ignorant or incompetent to get the document signed by a J.P. Illegitimate children pose a special problem and difficulties arise when men are supporting children without any legal obligation to do so (for instance, with no court order against them). Tax offices vary in their administration of the law regarding evidence of payment. Some accept postal order counterfoils, others insist on money order counterfoils, but the latter present difficulties, as in the case where the grandmother in rural Jamaica had a 3s. bus ride to try to cash the money order and then was unsuccessful. Insistence on proof of 'custody' of the child is another major stumbling-block. The greatest number of respondents who had failed to obtain tax relief, however, said that they had simply been refused tax relief by the tax office, but no explanation had been given to them.[1]

There were many complaints that forms had been completed and duly returned but there had been no reply from the tax office. One man, for instance, claimed to have obtained a form signed by a J.P. in Jamaica, from his wife in Jamaica, had sent in his marriage lines and birth certificate but at the date of the interview, some six weeks later, still had received no reply. Sometimes, of course, a hopeless case was presented: for example the man who was indignant because he could not get

---

[1] Another story is not infrequently told in Jamaica itself, that the necessary 'evidence' of support of children is sent from Jamaica for income tax purposes but the money fails to arrive. (See *West Indian Migrants*, p. 85 *et seq.*)

tax relief for his 'girl friend', or the man who felt he should get relief because he sends money occasionally to his sister's children. There is no doubt that tax offices have had many problems to deal with in this matter of immigrants and there is no question here of a general indictment of the efficiency, the courtesy or the fairness of most of the tax officials. They have a difficult job to do, and the law to administer, but many of their regulations were not designed to cope with the peculiar sociological problems of coloured immigrants.

Marriage, of course, is the best answer to many of these income tax problems, as many of the Jamaican men are now beginning to discover. The Jamaican High Commission in London gives advice and help on tax difficulties wherever it can when approached, but it can only touch the fringe of the problem. A case could be made out for the establishment of a specialist officer in the United Kingdom tax offices, to deal largely with coloured immigrants in order that their special problems may be handled with greater understanding than they are at present in some of the local tax offices.

*Savings*

Reference has already been made to the 'pardner', which was also investigated during the enquiry. This is a well-known Jamaican institution, which may be described as a temporary co-operative savings club. A typical 'pardner' (it is called a 'sou sou' in Trinidad and has other names in different parts of the West Indies) consists of five to twenty people, who agree to contribute perhaps between £1 to £5 a week to a common fund. Each week there is a draw, by ballot or agreement, so that each member in turn receives a lump sum of between £5 to £100 during the life of the 'pardner'. A trustworthy person takes the initiative in organizing the group, collecting the money and paying out the 'draw': it is unusual for this person to receive any formal payment for this service, but he would normally receive a gift from the recipient of the jackpot each week.

This system no doubt performs a useful service in rural Jamaica, where the common effort of regular savings enables people to accumulate money for lump-sum payments without getting involved in extortionate interest charges by private moneylenders or some hire-purchase companies. In England circumstances are different and it remains to be seen whether the 'pardner' will survive. (At the end of the first year after arrival 25 % of the persons questioned said that they were, or in the recent past had been, members of a 'pardner'.) In one case a man claimed still to be a member of a 'pardner' in Jamaica, but this was an unusual situation: typically it is organized on the basis of the household in England. A few, but very few, of the respondents said that they were saving in orthodox United Kingdom savings institutions such as the Post Office Savings Bank or a clothing club at work. Many said that they could not save anything at all. Some said they would join a 'pardner' if they could find one and could trust the other people in it to pay their contributions on the due date. Presumably an action for fraud would lie against a defaulter, but it may prove to be a matter of great practical difficulty to prosecute successfully for failure to observe such an informal agreement as the typical 'pardner', where there are normally no documents or records of any kind.[1] The urge to engage in some form of co-operative saving is strong amongst at least a substantial minority of the Jamaican community, but the 'pardner' may prove to be unsuitable for export, and traditional British institutions not adaptable enough. New approaches, such as the suggestion that credit unions (also familiar in Jamaica) should be started in England, have not been greeted with much enthusiasm[2] but perhaps, in time, new methods will be found of meeting a clear social need which calls for new institutions in a new environment.

[1] A report has been received that there was at least one case of such prosecution in Brixton.

[2] The first credit union amongst Jamaican migrants began in Hornsey in late 1963 and was registered the following year. By 1965 it was reported to have some 200 members and assets of about £2,000. This idea may quickly spread and become a new social force, provided it can surmount the inevitable problems which face any new organization in its early days.

## Chapter VII

## TEMPORARY OR PERMANENT
## MIGRATION

THE extent to which an immigrant population settles down in a new environment, and therefore the urgency with which the individuals seek to become integrated with that environment, are affected in part, but only in part, by their attitudes and expectations regarding the country from which they have emigrated. People who have moved as a consequence of some political upheaval, war or revolution are likely to have a different attitude towards returning home from those who emigrate for economic reasons. Coloured immigrants in Britain have moved in response to economic, rather than political, forces and the way they view an eventual return to their homeland will depend on their view of the future economic circumstances there. Their assessment of the possibilities of securing the financial means to return is another important factor, as is their expectation of the future for themselves, and their families, in Britain.

In trying to assess the extent of this desire to return to the homeland in Jamaica amongst the sample covered by the Jamaican Sample Survey seven criteria were selected for study as follows:

(1) continuing contact with Jamaica by correspondence;
(2) stated plan for return to Jamaica and the active steps taken to implement those plans;
(3) nationality of landlord;
(4) length of occupation of their current dwelling;
(5) plans about accommodation whilst in Britain;
(6) intention regarding children left behind in Jamaica;
(7) remittances to Jamaica.

At the end of the first year 27% of the men and 38% of the women said that they corresponded with their families in Jamaica at least once a week. After they had been in England for a further year, these proportions had dropped to 21% and 29% respectively. In the case of men 7% at the end of the first year, and 12% at the end of the second year, said that they corresponded with their families less than monthly: only 4%

said they never corresponded, whilst at the end of the second year virtually all the women claimed to be in touch with their families at least once a month.

Ties with friends, as might be expected, grew much less close as the length of stay in England extended. At the end of the first year 13 % of both men and women said they never corresponded with friends in Jamaica. This proportion had risen to 36% or 37 % at the end of the second year. At the end of the first year 48 % of the men and 54 % of the women claimed to correspond with friends at least once a month. At the end of the second year these proportions had fallen to 21 % and 27 % respectively (Table 49).

TABLE 49

*Contact with Jamaica (per cent)*

|  | Men | | Women | |
|---|---|---|---|---|
| Communicate with: | *After 1 yr.* | *After 2 yrs.* | *After 1 yr.* | *After 2 yrs.* |
| *Family* | | | | |
| Weekly or more often | 27 | 21 | 38 | 29 |
| Not weekly, at least monthly | 65 | 63 | 54 | 70 |
| Less than monthly | 7 | 12 | 8 | 1 |
| Never | 1 | 4 | — | — |
|  | 100 | 100 | 100 | 100 |
| *Friends* | | | | |
| Weekly or more often | 8 | — | 12 | 6 |
| Not weekly, at least monthly | 40 | 21 | 42 | 21 |
| Less than monthly | 39 | 43 | 32 | 36 |
| Never | 13 | 36 | 13 | 37 |
|  | 100 | 100 | 100 | 100 |

*Source:* Jamaican Sample Survey

One migrant claimed to post ten letters a week back to Jamaica, another produced a pile of letters from friends in Jamaica and said he kept up a regular correspondence with them as well as with his family. Very often long hours of work rather than the lack of desire hinder correspondence—in one case a school teacher from Jamaica said that the teachers and pupils from the school she had left were writing to her, but she had no time to reply until she was ill, when she wrote sixty letters home. A few, but not many, had received no schooling and were therefore unable, unaided, to correspond with anyone. One respondent said that she wrote home only when she had some news, but often for weeks at a time there was nothing to write about. The general impression is one of a weakening link with Jamaica, except in the case of women corresponding with families where, after a two-year absence, the contact was still very close.

Distance lends enchantment, and to ask a Jamaican in the middle of an English winter whether or not he would like to return to Jamaica would be the most futile enquiry imaginable. The problem faced in this investigation was to try to untangle from the web of confused ideas which most people entertain about their future, to what extent the Jamaicans being interviewed had serious intentions of returning to their homeland 'one day'. Whether they will, in fact, ever do so is beside the point. What matters now, as the motivation towards any kind of cultural assimilation with the English community, is whether they feel it is worth while making the effort, quite apart from the likelihood of success. Our sample were therefore asked the straight question: 'Would you like to return to Jamaica?' As expected, the vast majority said 'Yes', although it was a little surprising to find that one man in five and one woman in ten, at the end of their second year, said 'No'. If the reply was 'Yes', then two further questions followed: did they intend to return within the next five years, or at some indefinite future time, and had they saved any money towards the return fare?

The results of this enquiry in each of two successive years are given in Table 50. At the end of the first year 74% of the men and 86% of the women said that they intended to return to Jamaica 'some time'. By the end of the second year this proportion had increased to 81% for men and 89% for the women, which suggests that the group had made little or no progress towards settling down in England. The simple expression of a desire to return is not too reliable a guide—there must be few migrants to any country who, in the earlier years, do not feel a nostalgia for home. A more useful guide, perhaps, is the proportion who said that they intended to return within the next five years. At the end of the first year 23% of the men and 24% of the women who said they intended to return fell into this category. At the end of the second year the men in this group had increased to 30%, the women slightly decreased to 22%. Even this is not a fully reliable guide to real intention, as distinct from vague aspiration, although clearly a substantial proportion of the group regarded themselves very decidedly as birds of passage. At the end of the second year the question was asked: 'Have you saved any money towards your fare?' The replies revealed that 26% of the men and 16% of the women planning to return claimed to have saved some money for the purpose.

TABLE 50

*Plans for Return to Jamaica (per cent)*

|  | Men | | Women | |
|---|---|---|---|---|
| Plan to return | *First yr.* | *Second yr.* | *First yr.* | *Second yr.* |
| *Yes* | 74 | 81 | 86 | 89 |
| *No* | 26 | 19 | 14 | 11 |
|  | 100 | 100 | 100 | 100 |
| *Of those planning to return:* | | | | |
| In 5 years | 23 | 30 | 24 | 22 |
| Indefinite | 77 | 70 | 76 | 78 |
|  | 100 | 100 | 100 | 100 |
| Money saved | — | 26 | — | 16 |
| No money saved | — | 73 | — | 84 |
|  | 100 | 100 | 100 | 100 |

*Source:* Jamaican Sample Survey

The comments of some of the individuals included in the statistics are illuminating. One young man explained how, though his parents do not plan to go back to Jamaica, he does. He misses his old job and his friends, saying that he was never keen to come to England in the first place and only made the move because his family were all over here—he is anxious to return as soon as he can. This case illustrates a tendency for migration to be infectious—it became the 'vogue' in Jamaica to go to England in the period before 1962, and many migrants just followed the crowd. One woman was emphatic and very resentful that economic circumstances in Jamaica forced her to leave and come to a country she hates and where she is unhappy. One man living in a large apartment house said that had he known how hard life was in England he would not have come, and he is determined to prevent his daughter, now in Jamaica and wanting to come to England, from migrating. He argued that he could not afford to keep her in England and he does not think it right that she should let the Government do so, as jobs are difficult to get.

There were some pathetic case histories recorded in the survey. One visitor reported that the man she interviewed was the type of person who accepts fate and suffers in silence. He was obviously miserable and lonely, living in one room and looking after himself. He was very keen that his girl friend should join him, but he accepted in good faith her misinformed statement that she could not come after 1 July 1962 (when the Commonwealth Immigrants Act came into operation) and spent the money he had saved for her fare. One woman welcomed the visitor with a cup of tea—a mark of cultural assimilation?—and was described as a 'warm, pleasant woman, easy to talk to'. She had been very homesick and cried whenever she had a letter from her mother. She said she would like to go home but did not know how she would get her fare. This was a constantly recurring theme in many of the reports—not a few replied that they would catch the next plane if only they could find the fare. Others were determined to make the best of it and then go home. A typical case was a man described as young, intelligent and unattached who intended to get some training as quickly as possible and then return home. Others sink into apathy. Mrs. R. seemed tired and disorganized. She would like to be back in Jamaica but is not doing anything about it. She would like her child to come to England but again is not making much effort. The room was clean and tidy except for a pile of clothes waiting to be ironed on the bed. Her clothes were very shabby and not very clean. These are cases picked from dozens of such reports as illustrative of the human problem, submerged and largely unknown, brought about by the migration.

Not all the reports were so gloomy: one or two, but not many, replied that they would like to return to Jamaica for a holiday only. Many of them were clear that they would return permanently only if they had made a success of life in England and could return with some financial evidence of that success. A minority expressed grave concern about the economic conditions in Jamaica and were on the whole pessimistic about the future. One man, for example, thought he might return to Jamaica in ten years or so, but only if employment improved in that island. 'No use to sit in the sun and laugh', he explained.

There were success stories too. Mr. H., described as a 'very jolly, happy man, bursting with ideas and enterprise', had transferred a very flourishing tailoring business from Jamaica to England and was doing very well, having spent six months in the United States to see if he liked it there. He left Jamaica, he said, because he was thoroughly disgusted with the Jamaican Government which, he alleged, is only encouraging large-scale firms from outside, neglecting Jamaicans who are struggling to 'get on their feet'. Even so, he ran a big car in England, and had a house and two workshops, whilst actively looking for bigger premises to house his expanding staff. He was unusual, and was the only example noted in the enquiry of a successful self-employed small businessman. Other successful cases could be quoted, but two will suffice as illustration. Mr. S. knows exactly what he wants, and does not want to go back to Jamaica. He wants to get his wife over as he feels she would learn so much and that there are opportunities for her in nursing. Mrs. C. came to England with the intention of getting married and was in fact married in an Anglican church in September 1961. Her husband works as a mechanic, she has experience as a hairdresser; she does some work privately at the weekend but wants to get further training. Mr. C. is studying at night school to become an engineer. They are thinking of buying a car, then a house (in that order), and are apparently thoroughly content with life in England.

It is often assumed that immigrant groups tend to cluster together in particular residential areas and that as a result they tend to retard the process of integration. This general assertion, which is widely believed, is capable of several interpretations. One important aspect of this tendency to huddle together in social groups based upon a common national origin is the extent to which immigrants are living as tenants in houses with a landlord of the same, or different, nationality. No information can be derived from the Census on this point, but during the two-year study of Jamaican immigrants information was collected at the end of the first year, then at the end of the second year, which throws some light on this matter so far as Jamaicans are concerned.

At the end of the first year, three-quarters of the persons covered by the survey were living in houses as tenants of Jamaican landlords (almost one in five were living with a Jamaican *relative* as a landlord). At the end of the second year the position had hardly changed at all—the numbers living with Jamaican landlords had fallen slightly, by about 4%, whilst the proportion of Jamaican relatives had increased and that of non-relatives had fallen. At the end of the first year one in twenty of the households had an English landlord: at the end of the second year this proportion had increased to one in ten. Relatively few (5% in the second year) had other West Indians as landlords, the same proportion as for Asians. The results were quite conclusive—the great majority of the Jamaicans in the survey are 'clustering' in largely Jamaican households, but it is not clear whether this is from choice or necessity. (See Table 51.)

## TABLE 51

### *Nationality of Landlord (per cent)*

| Nationality of landlord | End of first year | End of second year |
|---|---|---|
| Jamaican relative* | 18 | 22 |
| Jamaican non-relative | 59 | 51 |
| Jamaican | 77 | 73 |
| English | 6 | 10 |
| Others, including | 17 | 17 |
| | 100 | 100 |
| West Indians (non-Jamaicans) | 3 | 5 |
| Asians† | 5 | 5 |
| Europeans‡ | 3 | 3 |
| Others, or own house or not specified | 6 | 4 |

*Source:* Jamaican Sample Survey

* The term 'relative' was not always clearly understood, although the words 'blood relative' were included in the question. Mostly it was interpreted as including close relatives by marriage, cousins or aunts recognized by the respondent as part of the 'family'.

† Mainly Indians and Pakistanis.              ‡ Mainly Poles and Italians.

As might be expected, the longer immigrants have been in Britain the longer they tend to have resided in their present accommodation. By the end of the second year of the enquiry, none of the individuals interviewed could have been in Britain for longer than three years, yet in many cases they joined households which were already established in Britain. Enquiries were made as to how long the *household* to which the immigrant belonged, as distinct from the immigrant himself, had been living in their existing accommodation. It was found at the end of the first year that about one-third of the families had been living at the same address for a year at least, but less than three years. One year later this proportion had risen to 50%. These figures are interesting in that they suggest a general tendency to settle down and not keep moving about. We found during our enquiries that one of our greatest administrative problems was to keep track of the changing addresses of our contacts, particularly in the first few months of their stay in Britain, as they moved from one address to another trying to find suitable accommodation (Table 52).

TABLE 52

*Length of Occupation (per cent)*

| Period of occupation of premises | End of first year | End of second year |
|---|---|---|
| Under 1 month | 5 | 7 |
| 1 month under 3 months | 11 | 11 |
| 3 months under 12 months | 43 | 32 |
| 12 months under 3 years | 34 | 50 |
| 3 years or over | 6 | — |
| | 100 | 100 |

*Source:* Jamaican Sample Survey

In order to provide yet a further check on this point questions were asked about plans for future accommodation whilst in Britain—did the individual intend to remain where he was or did he plan to move, and if so did he want to leave the district or not? The replies to this question varied considerably. Those who expressed a desire to move usually had some specific reason for wanting to make a change—to be nearer place of employment or study, or because the landlord would not repair the kitchen tap, were amongst the reasons given. Some respondents were under notice of eviction, perhaps over a dispute with the landlord, whilst one woman was concerned about the attitude of her landlord to the child she was expecting. One man had moved at least three times since reaching England but when attempts were made to find out the reasons he could not explain them—apparently he just takes it into his head to move. Others were more or less content; they would like more room for the baby to crawl, or felt that their rent was too high, but had not taken any definite steps towards finding alternative accommodation.

The wide variety of the replies can be summarized by saying that almost three-quarters of the persons interviewed said that they intended to remain where they were for the time being, the remainder wanting to move. Of those who intended to move, a quarter proposed to buy property when they could (either because they want to settle down in Britain or because property is regarded as a promising speculative venture), half of them were not interested in buying property and a quarter were un-decided. Just under a half of those intending to change their accommodation wanted to remain in the same district, whilst a quarter wanted to leave the district (Table 53).

TABLE 53

*Plans about Accommodation whilst in Britain*

|  | Per cent |
|---|---|
| Intend to remain in present accommodation | 71 |
| Do *not* intend to remain | 29 |
|  | 100 |
| Of those *not* intending to remain: |  |
| Planning to buy | 23 |
| Not planning to buy | 50 |
| No stated plans | 27 |
|  | 100 |
| Want to leave the district in which they are now living | 26 |
| Do *not* want to leave district | 43 |
| No clear reply | 31 |
|  | 100 |

*Source:* Jamaican Sample Survey

It is possible to make use of statistics obtained from the Census to throw some light on the extent to which persons changed their addresses in the year immediately preceding the Census. The persons included in the 10% of the population who were required during the Census to complete the full schedule were asked to give their usual address at the time of the Census in April 1961. They were then later asked if the address they had given was their usual address a year previously (that is, on 23 April 1960). The respondents could then be classified into two groups according to whether they had, or had not, changed their usual residence in the year preceding the Census. Persons entering Britain for the first time in that year would be regarded as having changed their address; thus figures were obtained relating to persons enumerated at their usual residence showing the numbers who had changed their usual residence during the year previous to the Census. These figures were analysed by the computer for the present enquiry into the eight groups based upon the birthplace of the individual, again drawing a random one-in-twenty-five sample when the respondent stated that he or she was born in England.

We know the number of persons enumerated in the sample in the twenty-eight metropolitan boroughs in the eight selected birthplace groups, and we know the number of those persons who stated that they had changed their residence in the year preceding the Census. By calculating percentages in each case, we can compare the recorded experiences of the different groups as in Table 54.

TABLE 54

*Residential Mobility of Birthplace Groups*

| Persons born in | Number of persons in the sample | Percentage who changed residence in year preceding the census |
|---|---|---|
| England | 10,391* | 9 |
| Jamaica | 2,992 | 36 |
| Caribbean | 2,600 | 42 |
| India | 2,529 | 28 |
| Pakistan | 361 | 35 |
| Poland | 2,171 | 11 |
| Ireland | 14,118 | 24 |
| Cyprus | 2,063 | 28 |
| All metropolitan boroughs | 37,225 | 22 |

*Source:* 10% Census analysis

\* 1 in 25 sample.

From the point of view of residential mobility, the persons born in England show the least record of movement, for only about one person in ten changed residence in the year preceding the Census. The persons born in Poland are almost as stable. At the other extreme persons born in the British West Indies (Caribbean area) other than those born in Jamaica seem to be the most mobile, for two persons out of five changed their residence in the year. The Jamaicans and the Pakistanis seem to be about equally mobile, with about one person in three recording a change of residence: the Indians and the Irish also seem to have about the same record of movement, being in the region of one mover in four persons. Taking the metropolitan boroughs as a whole, we can see that almost one person in five of these eight different groups changed residence in the year before the Census. If we ignore the English groups the proportion amongst the immigrant groups rises to 27%—over one mover in four persons.

### Children

In an earlier study[1] it was estimated that 98% of the children of the migrants from Jamaica were left behind. It was also suggested that the persons migrating in 1961 were not a typical cross-section of the Jamaican population, in that it then appeared that the number of children per 100 adults recorded during the sample enquiry was higher than in the population of Jamaica as a whole. This observation has been confirmed by the publication of more recent statistics by the Government of Jamaica which have been derived from the 1960 Census in that island. In that year the Census takers recorded 634,705 persons aged fourteen years and under, 974,721 over fourteen years of age: a total of 1,609,426 persons altogether living in the island of Jamaica, which means that there were 65 children per 100 adults in the island as a whole. It had been shown in the previous study that 90% of the persons migrating from Jamaica interviewed during the enquiry were under forty years of age; if we therefore exclude persons over that age from our calculations we can say that in Jamaica in 1960 there were 592,741 persons in the age group fifteen to thirty-nine years, and thus there were 107 children per 100 adults in the age group fifteen to twenty-nine. Even recognizing that part of the discrepancy may be due to the size of the sample or qualities of response in both the sample enquiry and the Census, it still seems true to assert, on the basis of the only available evidence, that the migrants are

[1] *West Indian Migrants*, Table 31, p. 70.

not typical of their age group in Jamaica in that they appear to have appreciably larger families than their contemporaries in the island as a whole.

If we now turn to the evidence derived from the United Kingdom Census, it transpires that there were 6,284 children aged fourteen years and under recorded in Jamaican households in the seven London boroughs covered by that analysis. In those same households there were 14,694 persons aged between fifteen and forty years, an average of forty-three children per 100 adults in this age group living in Jamaican households in Britain. It is impossible to say, from Census data, how many children of the Jamaican adults enumerated still remain in Jamaica, but in the sample enquiry questions were asked to try to elucidate the number of children born in Britain, or brought to Britain by persons included in the sample and the number still remaining in Jamaica.

In the sample there were thirty-four children recorded as living in Britain in 1963, an average of eighteen children per 100 adults: this should be compared with the overall picture given by the United Kingdom Census of forty-three children per 100 adults in the child-bearing age group in Jamaican households. This is quite a considerable difference which may be due, in part, to sampling error or quality of response in either Census or sample or both, although it may be due to the fact that the Census data relate to Jamaican migrants who have been in Britain for a considerable time, as well as the more recent arrivals. Very often the first year or two after arrival is spent in getting a regular job and acquiring accommodation suitable for family occupation. One would expect, therefore, that the longer-period immigrants would have a higher proportion of children in Britain per 100 adults. What is not clear from the United Kingdom Census, which is concerned only with children resident in Britain, is how many children of the Jamaican migrants are still left in Jamaica. The evidence from the sample enquiry suggests that although the number of children left behind has dropped from 98% to 89% after a two-year interval, the number left behind is still quite high. The social problem left behind still exists in Jamaica and is still a major factor adversely affecting the happiness of Jamaican migrants to Britain and their children in Jamaica, although no official action has been taken either in Jamaica or in Britain to evaluate the problem or take any effective steps for dealing with it (Table 55).

TABLE 55

*Number of Children in Jamaica and Britain*

|  | Enquiry in Jamaica | Enquiry in Britain |
|---|---|---|
| Total number of children in both Jamaica and Britain | 547 | 303 |
| Adults included in the enquiry | 364 | 189 |
| Children per hundred adults | 150 | 160 |
| Left in Jamaica *Number* | 535 | 269 |
| Living in Britain *Number* | 12 | 34 |
| Per cent left in Jamaica | 98 | 89 |

*Source:* Jamaican Sample Survey

The existence of so many children left behind in the island of Jamaica means that the United Kingdom Census taken by itself is of very little use for studying the family structure of Jamaicans in Britain. It also means that direct comparisons between, say, the English households and the Jamaican households must be made with great circumspection in this regard. Equally it is not possible to draw any valid conclusions from comparisons between different immigrant groups unless it is known what proportion of children have been left behind in the country of origin. Attempts to forecast the future trends of the different segments of the population growth are likely to be confounded if large numbers of children have been left behind by immigrants and then, in some cases but perhaps not in others, are brought over to join their parents in Britain over the next few years.

The immigrants' intention regarding leaving children in Jamaica or bringing them to the United Kingdom is clearly of relevance in trying to decide how far the immigrants are settling and wanting finally to transplant their families to Britain. Half the men and just over one-third of the women interviewed in the present study had no children in Jamaica, but of those with children still in Jamaica at the end of the two-year period 20% of the men and 24% of the women intended to bring the children over to join them in the United Kingdom as soon as possible, whereas 14% of the men and 26% of the women were undecided or made no reply. This means that two-thirds of the men and half of the women with children had no intention of bringing their children to Britain.

The difficulty here is to put a precise interpretation on the word 'intention'. It could be that many of the people replying in the negative would bring their children over if they could, but see no prospect of doing so for financial reasons or because of housing difficulties. These replies, therefore, cannot be taken as an expression of desire. Indeed many times reports were received of the great distress felt by the parents concerning their children and yet they felt unable to surmount the formidable obstacles in the way of a family reunion. A few—but probably very few—are reconciled to a permanent separation and do not expect to see their children again. In the majority of cases it seems reasonable to assume that the parents intend to rejoin the children in Jamaica rather than the other way round. Most of the negative replies were not elaborated, but three clearly distinct subdivisions can be discerned in the remainder of the replies. In some cases the parents would like to bring the children over but are prevented from doing so because of lack of accommodation in England, no money to pay the fare, no way of finding an adult escort for the child on the journey or, in a few cases, difficulties over the Commonwealth Immigrants Act.[1] In other cases the children seem happily settled in Jamaica with grandmother or other relative, perhaps the mother, and the parent does not wish to disturb them. In others, not more than half a dozen altogether, the adult so dislikes living in England (the weather being a constant source of complaint) that he would not bring his children over to suffer what he himself is suffering (Table 56)!

The replies which indicated a desire to bring the children but where the individual is frustrated are often very revealing. Miss X., for example, had no definite plans for bringing her son over but would like him to come if circumstances allowed it. She insisted that she came to the United Kingdom to work and otherwise would return to Jamaica, as she hates England. She believed, however, that by the time she can afford to go back she will be too old to get a good job in Jamaica, though she was taking commercial courses here—a new generation will have arisen in Jamaica and taken all the best jobs, she argued. A very

[1] This was written before the severe restrictions imposed in August 1965.

## TABLE 56

*Intentions regarding bringing Children to the United Kingdom*
*(per cent)*

|  | Men | Women |
|---|---|---|
| No children in Jamaica | 51 | 38 |
| With children in Jamaica | 49 | 62 |
|  | 100 | 100 |
| *Of those with children in Jamaica:* | | |
| (1) Intend to bring to U.K. | 20 | 24 |
| (2) Do *not* intend to bring to U.K. | 66 | 50 |
| (3) Undecided or no reply | 14 | 26 |
|  | 100 | 100 |

*Source:* Jamaican Sample Survey

different case is that of Mr. H., who was negotiating to move his whole family and his tailoring business to England. His car and sewing-machine had already arrived, and his family were expected about three months later. Some respondents specifically indicated that they wanted the children to join them because they would get a better education and chance in life in England; some reported difficulties in getting documents and even plane seats; others mentioned the problem of escorts. Sometimes relatives in Jamaica objected to parting with the children, but this was mentioned in only isolated cases.

The complex pattern of marital and non-marital relations observed during this enquiry reinforces what has been stated many times about the general disorganization of family life in Jamaica, to which this recent migration to Britain has added further confusion. The fact is that it is quite usual for a mother to leave her children with their grandmother in the rural areas while she herself gets a job in Kingston, while the men in Jamaica frequently have to migrate in search of work. The idea of leaving children with their grandmother for an extended period has, over the years, become an accepted pattern of social behaviour (just as some people in England leave their children for extended periods in boarding schools) and therefore the break caused by the migration to England is not as much of a shock as English observers might expect. Nevertheless the fragmentation of family life in this way must have profound effects on rural social structure. It is against this background that the persistent efforts towards what is called 'community development' in Jamaica must be viewed.

Remittances from migrants to Britain have been an important element in the invisible balance of payments of Jamaica in recent years[1] and a high proportion of the migrants in the sample were sending remittances back to Jamaica. This point has been discussed more fully in the chapter dealing with household budgets but it may be noted here, in passing, that there is no evidence from the present investigation of a weakening of the link with Jamaica, judged by the proportion of income remitted to Jamaica. The amount sent varies according to income category, but in three out of four income categories the proportion of income remitted to Jamaica was higher at the end of the second year than at the end of the first year (see Table 46).

What general conclusions can we draw from this analysis? We can reasonably say that it could easily apply to migrants in general. It may well be that similar investigations amongst any group of migrants anywhere—say Pakistanis in Britain or English in Canada—would produce similar results. Once the excitement of the journey and transplantation are over, the hard realities of the new life become much plainer and the glow of memory warms the heart towards the homeland, time and distance blunting the recollection of the pressures that led to migration. Perhaps any group of migrants would tend to draw in on themselves, strengthen their ties with their homeland, the family acting as a defensive mechanism against what is perceived to be a hostile environment. Nevertheless there is a feeling widely current amongst social workers in Britain today that West Indians as a group can be differentiated sharply from other coloured immigrants (for instance, Pakistanis and Indians) because, it is felt, the former more than the latter desire to be integrated with the British community. This view is widely held because the language barrier is much less for West Indians and because a minority of local West Indian leaders—and their political leaders in the West Indies—have stated that this *ought* to be their desire.

The evidence so far adduced indicates that this view must be

---

[1] According to the official Economic Survey of Jamaica in 1963, in that year Jamaican migrants to Britain sent £7·3 million back to Jamaica, £7·8 million in 1962 and £7·1 million in 1961.

reconsidered. On each of the four criteria so far examined there is no evidence that Jamaicans, in the early years of their stay in Britain, show any strong inclination to sever their ties with Jamaica. If anything the evidence points the other way—there is a strengthening, not a weakening, of the links. If this is indeed the case, several important questions of policy arise. Will this observed tendency be reversed with time? Will the time come when the migrants accept that they are permanently in the United Kingdom or will they continue their efforts to return to the lands of their origin? Will it be left for the second and third generations to make the fundamental psychological changeover? Will the children born in Britain be brought up to regard themselves first as Jamaicans destined one day to return 'home'? If this strong link with the homeland persists through time, perhaps even to subsequent generations, what ought public policy to be? Should the efforts made in the last decade, fully supported by political leaders in the West Indies, to integrate the West Indians into British society and thus to discourage any large-scale return to the islands be continued and expanded, and if so in what way? Alternatively, should it be accepted that for many years to come West Indian migrants will resist attempts at integration, not consciously or vociferously, but by quietly ignoring any efforts to weaken the links with their homeland and turn their minds positively towards seeking a new permanent relationship, co-operative if possible, competitive if not, towards the host community? It may be that some compromise solution will be found—that the immigrants will retain close links with their home countries (for instance, by periodic visits on holiday, maintaining correspondence, or sending cash back to dependants) and a close contact with the homeland of a sentimental kind, such as the Irish emigrants to the U.S.A. retain for Ireland, and this sentiment will not necessarily prevent a full acceptance of a new way of life in Britain.

# Chapter VIII

## THE PROCESS OF INTEGRATION

IT is not our present purpose to discuss whether the aim of policy in Britain today, so far as its coloured population is concerned, should be to integrate, assimilate, tolerate or repatriate the coloured community, or whether some variation on one or more of these themes can or should be adopted. Opinions may differ widely, not only on the precise meaning of these terms but also upon the means by which any agreed policy should be pursued. Our present task is more limited. Granted that the coloured immigrants have arrived in Britain, to what extent and by what processes are they in fact being 'integrated' or absorbed into the existing British social organization?

The integration of the coloured immigrants into existing British society can be accomplished only if there is sufficient impetus to achieve this social integration by both the host community and the immigrant group. If either, or both, are determined to remain separate on a basis of mutual coexistence and tolerance or, at the other extreme, as mutually antagonistic groups, then integration in any meaningful sense is impossible. In practice, the situation is not as finely delineated as that. In both the host and the immigrant communities there are people who are apparently implacably opposed to any form of voluntary mingling of the races on any level, and in both there are individuals who desire at least some form of social integration. A comprehensive study of the process of social integration would, therefore, require an analysis of the tendencies and changing dynamics of the situation amongst all the groups in the community. In this study attention is directed to only part of the field, that of Jamaican immigrants, in an attempt to perceive the process of social integration into existing organized social groups as seen from their angle, and an attempt is made, on the basis of the sample enquiry, to arrive at some statistical measurement of some of the parameters in the complex equation of social variables with which we are dealing, supplemented by appropriate case material, in an endeavour to elucidate, by example, some of the elements in the whole process.

It is impossible to categorize people too rigidly when trying to assess their attitude to integration but we can, conceptually, distinguish as extreme those who positively seek to integrate from those who take the opposite, negative view. There is a third, 'conditional' category consisting of those people who, whilst cautiously willing to move towards some measure of integration, have certain mental reservations. In the nature of the case the objectors and the cautious tend to be more specific about their attitudes. Those who want to integrate into the existing society demonstrate their desires more by their actions than by their words and probably have never stopped to reflect that they are, in fact, adopting a particular attitude to this question. The greater part of this chapter will be concerned with the large majority of the group interviewed who can be regarded as 'positive' in some degree, although as we shall see they face many obstacles which differ between individuals and, for the same person, at different periods of time. Amongst the 'conditional' group, the great majority were those who said in the course of the interviews that they would like to join in some sort of social activity but were reluctant to make the first move —they were waiting for someone to take the initiative and invite them. Here are a few typical comments from interviewers which exemplify this attitude:

He is interested but has made no steps to join a club.

They have a club at the church but he hasn't been asked or encouraged to join.

Wouldn't go to a club on her own but if she knew someone who went and they invited her, she would go with them.

Vaguely interested in playing in the works cricket team.

Would be quite willing and welcome being asked to join social society. So far he has not been approached by any society or church.

Is lonely and would dearly like to join a social club of any kind so long as West Indians are welcome there, where he can meet people and enjoy life.

If an English person were to encourage him to join a local society and take him around he would be happy, but will not go ahead and do this on his own.

These are only a few of about fifty similar comments received—taken together they present a picture of many lonely people waiting for someone to take the initiative in welcoming them to participate in a wider social life. No doubt these individuals are no worse off in this respect than most newcomers to large cities anywhere, but it is an easy matter for them to assume that the comparatively little interest shown in them is because of their race and colour.

About thirty of the respondents could be classified as negative, in the sense that they showed no interest at all in taking part in any kind of organized social life outside their immediate homes. One man explained that it is better for coloured people to 'keep themselves to themselves', outside working hours; some prefer to stay at home and not take part in social life outside it; others felt that their church allegiance precluded any other kind of organized social contact. Some were plainly unsociable by any standard. 'I don't stand for clubs', one woman explained, 'and try to keep myself to myself. No one tells lies on you then.'

In many cases the real attitude to social integration is revealed when the obstacles to it, genuine or imagined, are discussed. The major 'obstacle', if that is the correct designation, preventing many Jamaican immigrants from establishing closer contact with white organized society is their preoccupation with their family and domestic life. As one woman put it, with conviction, she had 'too much on her brains with six children' to bother about clubs. Women with young children—particularly if they have to go to work—are often completely preoccupied by domestic matters. Sometimes, as might be expected, the husband or wife wanted to go out while the other one wanted to stay at home. In one house were found three married couples related to each other, where life was centred on the home, in an atmosphere of much teasing and laughing. They were not likely to be the 'clubbable' types. Others, too, were content just to stay at home, listen to the radio and talk to friends.

Poor health was mentioned occasionally as a reason for the absence of any kind of social contact, and many of the people interviewed complained that they had either no energy or no time for any kind of organized social activity. The existence of counter-attractions centred on the home in many cases militates against any form of social mixing with either the coloured or the white persons in the neighbourhood.

Goes to bed at 8 p.m. Gets to work at 7 a.m. and has to do her washing, etc., when she goes home, so goes to bed.

Isn't interested in societies—finds working odd shifts doesn't give him time to go regularly to clubs or night school as he sometimes works late.

Doesn't want to join any club, seems to have access to plenty of friends without clubs.

Has enough friends and can't be bothered.

The fact is that, like the majority of English people, very many of the migrants are perfectly content to do their job and find their amusement with a close circle of friends. They feel no urge to 'integrate' with white or coloured organized clubs or societies outside their immediate circle.

There were those who gave reasons for their deliberate avoidance of social contact with English people from psychological feelings of fear, lack of desire, reticence or lack of knowledge. Only one person stated explicitly that he avoided social contact for fear that the English and coloured would fight: one explained that he would not go to church because he felt that he would not hear what the rector was saying! Occasionally it was confided that fear of a rebuff (particularly in church) was a powerful factor preventing church attendance. There is evidence of a considerable natural reticence. One couple were described by a visitor as '. . . shy and reserved, but sincere, and I do not think they would wish to give false information'. A woman living alone was described as 'too shy to become a member of our society, and she would like to; hesitant about going to a strange church, does not wish to be rebuffed'. Lack of knowledge was widespread. Time and again migrants explained their apparent unwillingness to attempt to make any inroad into a wider social circle by claiming that they had no knowledge of any organization in the area which they could join. 'Would like to join a Pentecostal church but doesn't know how to find one and is not interested in other types of church', was a typical comment in a number of cases. People resident in an area for a length of time find it hard to comprehend how difficult it might be for the recently arrived coloured immigrant to find his feet in strange surroundings.

By what mechanism is the process of social integration being assisted or hindered? The hundreds of interviews conducted during this enquiry cast a certain amount of light on this question. One generalization *can* be made and that is that the social horizons of the immigrants are normally extremely limited. Quite a number appear to have no organized social life at all: they live alone and their contact with other human beings seems to be reduced to the bare minimum. Another group, considerably in the majority, do have some form of social life, but this is limited to people they meet at work (by far the most often quoted source of social contact) or in the neighbourhood. The majority, whilst expressing no animosity towards the white neighbours surrounding them, clearly indicated that they preferred the company of 'their own kind', meaning Jamaicans. People from the other West Indian islands such as Grenada or Antigua were classed, along with Africans, as friendly, but not intimate, contacts. Very little evidence of racial animosity appeared but where it did it was usually directed against 'Indians', which probably included Pakistanis also.

The most intensely personal relationship, the sexual, can be both a help and a hindrance to social integration for the family as a whole. Occasionally, but not often, reference would be made to an English relative by marriage and he or she was usually the principal link between her coloured family and the white population in the neighbourhood. Casual sexual relationships were not reported frequently but they do occur and no doubt existed far more often than they were reported. Mr. Y., for example, soon after his arrival in England, was approached in a public house by a white girl who invited him to a party (he bought the drinks) and the girl came to live with him. He was happy with her and they were, he thought, living a 'cosy life' but periodically she went away to stay with her 'mother'. She always returned until after a two-week absence he saw her drunk in the public house and she abused him. Having discovered that she was a prostitute, although he still cares for her, he is disgusted and lonely. He still wants a white girl—'no more Jamaican girls'—yet he believes that all English girls are loose-living. He meets them only in the public houses of suburban London and is desperately anxious to meet a 'nice' white girl.

Such cases are frequent, for by and large the philosophy of 'keep myself to myself' prevails amongst the coloured immigrants unless the white society around them is prepared to take the initiative, which is not often the case.

This, of course, is not universally true. One girl explained that her boy friend asked an Irish workmate home for Sunday dinner (they often have a drink together) to taste Jamaican chicken, but the 'friend' declined on the ground that he feared he might be poisoned! His attitude was in sharp contrast with that of the English neighbour, who was always helpful, especially when the Jamaican family moved next door. He met them at the station, helped with transport and generally created goodwill. Perhaps the most typical family can be portrayed as having mainly Jamaican friends who are either related or were usually known previously in Jamaica; few and only slight contacts with other West Indians; no contact with non-West Indian coloured people; and very little with white people— even with those living in the same house or street.

Casual meetings were frequently mentioned—when asked how they met a *Jamaican* friend the answer not infrequently was 'on the bus' or 'in the street'. Occasional contacts are made in the market, in the shops, in church or in some local sports club, but by far the most frequently mentioned medium of social contact between different races was the workplace. Time and again it transpired that the only social contact which the Jamaican has with the Englishman, which involves any kind of communication between them, arises from the workplace, a social contact which only occasionally appears to extend outside working hours.

During the enquiry everyone was asked if he or she had any English friends. Because of the difficulty of defining 'friends', those who replied in the affirmative to this question were then asked a supplementary, 'Have you ever been in an English home?' The results of this enquiry are summarized in Table 57, from which we may conclude that social contact between men tends to be more frequent than between women (work being the main element in the situation). Over half of each sex claimed to have English friends, and the number invited into an English home is not insignificant. One wonders how this would compare with the social contacts of other immigrant groups: how many Irish, or Poles, for instance, have visited English homes?

## TABLE 57

*Social Contacts (per cent)*

|  | End of second year | |
| --- | --- | --- |
|  | *Men* | *Women* |
| Social contact with English people |  |  |
| YES | 69 | 53 |
| NO | 31 | 47 |
|  | 100 | 100 |
| *Of those replying YES:* |  |  |
| Been in an English home | 61 | 50 |
| *Not* been in an English home | 39 | 50 |
|  | 100 | 100 |

*Source:* Jamaican Sample Survey

(No clear reply was received from two men and four women.)

Most Jamaican migrants arrive in England with a strong church tradition; the home social life of many was based upon the revivalist, Pentecostal type of church in Jamaica, not infrequently the offshoot of some American Negro sect—the Church of God, in its many variations, is predominant. Jamaica is subjected to a continuous stream of visiting evangelists, white and coloured, from the United States, who not infrequently conduct a revivalist campaign and leave behind them another church sufficiently demarcated from the next one by some fine point of doctrine, ritual or personalities to ensure the loyalty of the particular congregation—perhaps until the next evangelist appears. The more established denominations such as the Baptists or Methodists and, more recently, the Seventh Day Adventists, are strongly entrenched in all parts of Jamaica with a type of service reminiscent of the Southern States of the United States. It is against this background that the Jamaican migrant to Britain views his churchgoing in England and explains why so many of them find it difficult to adjust themselves to the relatively cold formality of an English church service.[1]

An attempt was made during our enquiry to find out what proportion of the sample were active members of some voluntary society at the end of the first year. Once the preponderance

[1] This comment was prepared before the publication of the Rev. Clifford Hill's book on *West Indian Migrants and the London Churches*, London, O.U.P. for the Institute of Race Relations, 1963.

of the church had been established by the first enquiry, at the end of the second year attention was directed to church attendance. The results of these related enquiries showed that almost half of the men and just over half of the women claimed to attend church of some kind. The majority were attending a conventional, established English church with a mixed congregation, but a sizeable minority (almost a quarter of the women) were attending churches which were composed almost exclusively of coloured people in the Pentecostal type of service (Table 58).

## TABLE 58

### Membership of Voluntary Societies

| | Per cent in membership at end of first year | |
|---|---|---|
| | Men | Women |
| Church (largely English) | 26 | 36 |
| Church (largely West Indian) | 14 | 22 |
| Co-operative society | 3 | 2 |
| Social/sports club (English) | 5 | 2 |
| Social/sports club (W.I.) | 5 | — |
| Political party | 2 | — |
| Education and training class | 13 | 11 |
| *Offices held in these societies* | | |
| Percentage holding some voluntary office | 2 | 1 |

*Source:* Jamaican Sample Survey

At the end of the second year the question of church membership was pursued in more detail. There was little change in the general pattern: 44% of the men (as against 40% in the first year) claimed a church connection, whilst among the women the proportions were 57% in the second year as against 58% in the first year. The great majority of the respondents attended a church meeting held in a recognized church building but a few of them were meeting in large houses or school halls, the main aim of all these little groups being to acquire sufficient funds to erect or purchase a building of their own (Table 59).

To what extent is the church aiding the social integration of the different races? This is an almost impossible question to answer unless one is prepared to assume that physical presence in the congregation on repeated occasions is a proof of social integration. The situation varies widely from individual to

TABLE 59

*Church Attendance (per cent at end of second year)*

|  | Men | Women |
|---|---|---|
| Attend church regularly | 44 | 57 |
| Do *not* attend church regularly | 56 | 43 |
|  | 100 | 100 |
| *Of those attending church:* | | |
| In a church building | 92 | 88 |
| In private house, school hall, etc. | 8 | 12 |
|  | 100 | 100 |

*Source:* Jamaican Sample Survey

(No clear reply was received from 1 man and 1 woman. The following denominations were principally mentioned, number of references in brackets: Church of God (several distinct sects quoted) (27), Baptist (22), Anglican (20), Methodist (5), Roman Catholic (5). Others were: Seventh Day Adventist, Pentecostal, Salvation Army, Congregational, Christadelphian, Apostolic Church, Pilgrim Holiness and Jehovah's Witnesses.)

individual and from church to church. One couple explained that they were very happy in the (mixed) church they go to and were loved by the congregation where they feel very much at home. They have been invited to visit the minister's house— but they have not been yet! One woman explained a minority view by asserting that 'in England you can't be a Christian, you have to be a slave'. Whatever may be the positive effect of the racially mixed church on race relations, it can be asserted with some confidence that the Pentecostal churches are antipathetic to social cohesion but the division here is not between races as such, but between believers and non-believers, the saved and the unsaved. As Mrs. S. explained, 'believers' have great faith in the joys of a future life but little to offer in this life, where there are wars, conflicts and so many things a coloured woman cannot do because she is coloured. Most of the Pentecostal sects take an extremely puritanical view of most social intercourse outside the church itself: they have prayer meetings in each other's houses but activities outside the church would be frowned upon, except for the purpose of converting the unbelievers. They are therefore inimical to social integration— except for a relatively small number of white people who are prepared to accept the discipline of a predominantly coloured church and adopt the extrovert type of service to which the congregation is accustomed.[1]

Apart from the church, training and educational classes were the most frequently mentioned organized social groups which appealed to the persons interviewed. The educational system in Jamaica, despite quite rapid extension in recent years, is still gravely deficient today for children, and facilities for adult education, particularly in the rural areas, are very poor by comparison with British standards. The scarce educational resources available have to be spread thinly in Jamaica and many of the Jamaicans who have migrated to Britain have had little chance of formal schooling to higher than a most elementary level. The prospect of improving their economic position either in Britain or in Jamaica by educational means is therefore alluring, for about one in ten stated that they were taking part in some sort of further education, usually with a strong vocational bias. The women said that they were interested in typing, nursing, knitting and sewing classes. The men were interested largely in carpentry, metal-work, engineering or some subject closely allied with their vocational aspirations. There was no evidence of any interest at all in what might broadly be termed cultural educational facilities, such as art, literature or music. In this respect the migrants in this sample are not in any way different from the majority of the people in their income group and neighbourhood. Interest in these matters is usually the result of a higher education which has been denied to these migrants and to many of their white contemporaries.

Politics presented little attraction and very few recorded any interest in, far less active participation in, any of the United Kingdom political parties. Only one man claimed to be a member of the Labour Party, and the general attitude was that a coloured person is well advised to keep clear of the white man's politics. The migrants have had politics enough, in many cases, in their home islands. Very few seemed to have heard of the co-operative movement. They may, of course, shop in co-operative shops, but the ideology of the movement has made

---

[1] The detailed study of Pentecostal sects by Dr. Malcolm Calley was conducted concurrently with and independently of the present enquiry. His work *God's People* (London, O.U.P. for the Institute of Race Relations, 1965) appeared after the above words were written.

little, if any, impact on them. None mentioned working-men's clubs or institutes and very few made reference to any kind of sport, athletic or recreational club apart from the occasional works club. Not even cricket came much into the conversation, despite the fact that the West Indies cricket team was playing in a series of Test Matches in Britain whilst the interviews were being conducted. It is true that hundreds of West Indians were highly visible at many of the Test Matches, but they represented only a small fraction of the West Indian population in Britain today.

By far the most important area of social contact between the races is the workplace, rather than the home neighbourhood. At home a man or woman can, if he or she wishes, shut the door and 'keep himself to himself', but at work some form of social communication is usually imperative. It is here, where communication is unavoidable, that the most bitter hostilities may arise or the nascent friendships develop. Time and again, when the person interviewed was asked if he had English friends, the reply would refer to one or more individual contacts at work. Typical replies were as follows:

Has two Scottish friends, fellows from work. Has been out with them but not very frequently.

Social contacts at work only.

Work seems only contact with white community.

No social contacts except for one English girl whom she met at work.

Made friends with English people at work. Visits them as well.

It is beyond question that, so far as the majority of the members of this particular sample are concerned, they made little or no complaint about their relationships with their workmates, white or coloured, in reply to questions on the subject. It is true that some of them were not enthusiastic: they described relations as tolerable rather than affable, while others would recount specific cases of difficulty with some particular person. Some said they encountered difficulty in a previous job but were much happier in the present one. Others elaborated and explained how they joked with their fellows or made friends with them.

Where the replies indicated an indifferent situation the answer was usually couched in conditional terms: for example, 'Finds majority of workmates friendly, or at any rate, not actively unfriendly.' Other typical reports were:

Some good, some not so good.

Some English treat them well, some not so well, but he is trying to be happy in his surroundings.

People from different islands tend to stick together and not mix very well. She does see some Jamaicans who work on other floors, but as they have their lunch-time at different hours, she does not talk to them. Supervisor is white and quite nice.

Some like us, some don't.

Gets on well except two or three English who abuse coloured—many coloured in the factory.

This last quotation contains the key to the explanation of difficulties in a number of cases. So long as the coloured workers are in a minority and present no threat, real or imagined, to the position of the other established workers, difficulties rarely arise. Insecurity seems to lie at the root of bad race relations in the few places where these exist—fear and jealousy lead to friction. One coherent description of a situation where race relations are unsatisfactory was as follows:

He likes going to work and has happy friendships with the coloured workers there. There is no contact whatever between white and coloured; all stick together with their own. When I asked if there was not a single white man he is friendly with he said 'No! The white don't like the coloured. Whenever anything goes wrong they blame it on us—they call us black b——.' There is no direct conflict, simply silent hostility, and they only talk to each other whenever this is absolutely necessary in the course of the work. I asked if he would like to be friendly with the whites. He said 'Yes', but if a coloured man approaches a white on friendly terms he is called a black b—— to his face so this makes the coloured keep to themselves and not go out to the white. I asked him if this kind of thing upsets him. At first he said 'Yes', then he said 'No'; he is happy with his coloured friends.

In only one case, where out of 150 employees 25% were coloured, was any physical violence reported. After a fight both the coloured and the white man involved were discharged. One coloured man, incensed by insults, went to the police, who complained to the foreman—since when things have improved. Informants sometimes complained that they were picked on for the dirty or heavy jobs; in other cases the individual concerned was clearly of such an aggressive type that he or she would have trouble anywhere. One girl explained how, in the works canteen, some tables are expressly reserved for whites and if a new white girl sits with the coloured girl she is dragged away. The canteen supervisor here is very antagonistic to the coloured people; the informant now takes her own lunch as she cannot stand the atmosphere in the canteen.

An attempt was made to discover the extent to which the trade-union movement is having any impact on the situation. At the end of the second year all the persons interviewed were asked if they were members of a British trade union. Those who replied in the negative were asked if they had ever been asked to join a union. Nearly two-fifths of the men were members of a trade union, and nearly one-fifth of the women. These figures relate to people who had been in Britain no more than three years, many of them working in unskilled jobs (and probably non-unionized factories). Of course, as expected, none was an official, but a quite high percentage claimed to have attended a branch meeting. It might well be argued that these figures of trade-union membership are hopeful, especially as so few migrants bring any tradition of trade-unionism with them from Jamaica. It is possible that it is going to be in this field of human relationships that progress towards integration will be made (Table 60).

How do Jamaican migrants to Britain spend their leisure time? A number of questions were asked during the survey, the answers to which throw some light on this question. The most important single medium of entertainment outside the home is the cinema: over half the men in each year said they went habitually whilst the proportion of women going showed a sharp increase from the first to the second year. West Indian parties have apparently gained in popularity, and the number of both sexes regularly using public houses has also increased. At the end of the second year nearly half the men, but only one woman in ten, claimed to use the public house regularly. Very few attend sports meetings, dog or horse racing or bingo sessions. The numbers of both sexes using dance halls increased from the first to the second year (Table 61).

### TABLE 60

*Trade-Union Membership (per cent at end of second year)*

|  | Men | Women |
|---|---|---|
| Member of U.K. trade union | 39 | 17 |
| *Not* a member | 61 | 83 |
|  | 100 | 100 |
| *Of the T.U. members:* |  |  |
| Attended a branch meeting | 45 | 13 |
| *Not* attended a branch meeting | 55 | 87 |
|  | 100 | 100 |
| *Of the non-members:* |  |  |
| Been asked to join | 17 | 13 |
| *Not* been asked to join | 83 | 87 |
|  | 100 | 100 |

*Source:* Jamaican Sample Survey

(Unions mentioned more than once, number of references in brackets: T. & G.W.U. (10), N.U.R. (5), N.U.M. (3), Amalgamated Society of Wood-workers (2). 11 other unions were named only once. 16 people said they were members of unions but could not give the name of the union or produce any evidence of membership.)

### TABLE 61

*Uses of Leisure (per cent)*

|  | Men | | Women | |
|---|---|---|---|---|
| *Habitually using:* | *First year* | *Second year* | *First year* | *Second year* |
| (1) *Passive media* |  |  |  |  |
| Cinema | 53 | 57 | 35 | 51 |
| Sports meeting | 14 | 24 | — | 5 |
| Dogs and horses | 7 | 9 | 4 | 3 |
| (2) *Active media* |  |  |  |  |
| West Indian parties | 41 | 61 | 33 | 47 |
| Public house | 38 | 47 | 2 | 11 |
| Evening classes | 13 | 27 | 11 | 14 |
| Dance hall | 22 | 37 | 8 | 14 |
| Bingo | 6 | 13 | 2 | 9 |
| (3) *Nothing* | — | 8 | — | 23 |

*Source:* Jamaican Sample Survey

The greater part of leisure time is spent at home watching television, reading the Bible, religious magazines, comic strips or the popular newspapers. The radio plays an important part in the life of the migrants, but probably talking to friends, relatives or neighbours provides the main diversion. The football pools were mentioned occasionally, as was Battersea Fun Fair. Weddings play an important part in the social life of the coloured community. Games such as cards, ludo and dominoes (which are frequently an important social activity in rural Jamaica) were rarely mentioned. Now and again the odd man out appears, for instance the man who played a saxophone in a band, plays skittles, cricket, dances and is out with friends looking for 'kicks'. He belonged to a social club at the place of work and as there are no other coloured people there he is something of a pet and is very popular, a role he clearly plays to the full. Such cases were rare enough to excite comment; in the main life is mundane and presents little variety.

How far is this routine relieved during the annual vacation? To try to establish this a question was asked as to where the last holiday (vacation) had been spent. Over half the respondents simply stayed at home: a further quarter either had no holiday at all or spent it visiting friends in one of the cities where, presumably, life continues along much the same lines as it does at home. Apart from one individual who claimed to have spent a week in Paris, one can see little evidence of any originality in the use of holidays. They have come to England—but they see little or nothing of the country, apart perhaps from an occasional day trip. Even those who live in a London suburb appear to make little or no effort to avail themselves of the wealth of art galleries, parks, museums and other cultural amenities within reach. They do not know how to use them: but it is an open question whether they would respond to any organized attempts to persuade them to do so. A similar statement may, of course, be made about large numbers of people of the same income group in the same neighbourhood who were born in London. It is not suggested that Jamaican immigrants are in any way peculiar in this respect (Table 62).

The web of relationships we have so far discussed is complex and difficult to simplify. Each person is an individual with different reactions to a similar environment and a different set of problems. Nevertheless is it possible to reach any *general* conclusion from the enquiry to sum up the overall relationship of this sample of Jamaican migrants to their new environment?

## TABLE 62

*Last Vacation Period (per cent at end of second year)*

| Method of spending last vacation periods: | Men and Women |
|---|---|
| Stayed at home | 54 |
| No holiday last year | 14 |
| Sick or pregnant | 5 |
| Went to London, Birmingham or Manchester to visit friends or relatives | 14 |
| Day trips | 8 |
| Seaside | 3 |
| Other | 3 |
| | 100 |

*Source:* Jamaican Sample Survey

(12 respondents gave no clear reply. Amongst the 'other' categories were reported: attending a church convention, travelling on railway concession tickets, cycling, going to Paris for a week (works outing).)

At the end of the second year, and usually after a number of interviews conducted at some length over a fairly extended period of time, each interviewer was in a position to form a general judgement of the individual or household in their environment. The interviewer was therefore asked to make a final assessment of the situation as he or she saw it in six main fields: domestic life, housing, employment, church, English neighbours, and Jamaican neighbours. Within each of these categories the interviewer was given four alternative conditions and asked to give the best assessment possible of the category in which he or she would place the individual who had been interviewed:

(a)   The individual has no observable problems.
(b)   There are problems but there is reasonable hope of solution within the near future.
(c)   The problems are considerable and there is no immediate sign of solution.
(d)   Hopeless.

The replies received to this question were then consolidated and a separate matrix drawn up for each sex attempting to measure the degree of settlement resulting from the process of integration as developed so far. The matrices are given, in percentages, in Table 63.

## TABLE 63

*Degree of Settlement (per cent)*

### (a) MEN

*Placed in category*

|                     | A  | B  | C  | D  |     |
|---------------------|----|----|----|----|-----|
| Domestic life       | 61 | 19 | 19 | 1  |     |
| Housing             | 75 | 13 | 9  | 3  |     |
| Employment          | 71 | 18 | 9  | 2  | 100 |
| Church              | 74 | 3  | 10 | 13 |     |
| English neighbours  | 56 | 13 | 18 | 14 |     |
| Jamaican neighbours | 94 | 5  | 1  | 1  |     |

### (b) WOMEN

|                     | A  | B  | C  | D  |     |
|---------------------|----|----|----|----|-----|
| Domestic life       | 77 | 14 | 7  | 2  |     |
| Housing             | 69 | 16 | 14 | —  |     |
| Employment          | 74 | 10 | 14 | 1  | 100 |
| Church              | 62 | 5  | 11 | 22 |     |
| English neighbours  | 55 | 10 | 13 | 21 |     |
| Jamaican neighbours | 94 | 1  | 4  | 1  |     |

*Source:* Jamaican Sample Survey

The great majority of the men and the women were felt to be in a reasonable state of settlement regarding their Jamaican neighbours in England, but relations with the English neighbours are apparently much less satisfactory: nearly a quarter of the women were classified as having an unsatisfactory relationship with little or no apparent prospect of improvement. The women seem better off from the domestic point of view—almost one man in five was in an unsatisfactory condition without any apparent immediate hope of solution for his problems. Employment relationships for both sexes were either regarded as completely satisfactory or at least with reasonable prospects of a solution being found to any existing problems. Housing does not emerge as badly as one might have expected. In view of the highly unsatisfactory housing position of West Indians relative to other birthplace groups, one would have expected a very different result, and it would not have been difficult to understand if a high proportion had been registered as having great housing problems. This was not the case. The truth of the matter is that although in relative terms West Indians are badly placed in the housing field in England, most of them are better off than they would be at home in the West Indies, and they are not, therefore, so conscious of their deprivations. This situation will undoubtedly change as the migrants become more accustomed to the English way of life and the standards of housing demanded as of right by other members of the community.

## Chapter IX

## FLIGHT TO DISENCHANTMENT

THE following cases are the stories of some of the Jamaicans that I[1] met in the Passport Office in Jamaica, and met again in a different world at a later date in London. The names are fictitious but the cases are true, as also is the letter received in March 1965, four years after my first meeting with Mrs. Jones in the Passport Office in Jamaica.

### Mrs. Wilson

When the money for the fare to England arrived from Mrs. Wilson's husband, she was sick, desperate, and she spent it on other things. Mr. Wilson was very vexed and refused to send her any more. Although she had six children and a mother to care for, she worked again in Jamaica until she had 'saved up the remainder'. She had been working for fifteen years as a maid and felt that if only she could go to England for six years or so and then return she could 'make good'.

The six children were left with their grandmother in Jamaica and Mrs. Wilson joined her husband in England. She explained about 'Granny' in the following words:

She have plenty out there she have six, by the mercy of God help us to help her, for I have to pay for sheets, buy feed at the weekends for baby Jane. She asked me not to have another, you must not tell her, she would fret. I've been to the birth control clinic and still have her. She would fret.

Baby Jane was born in England ten months after Mrs. Wilson's arrival, but as soon as she could after her birth Mrs. Wilson returned to work. Jane is left downstairs with a young girl who is given £1 a week plus meals for looking after her. 'She's not really looking after her, she is real attentive babies, grants me that favour. She won't charge, we just give her, she is real attentive to her.' Content that all her children are well cared for, she obviously does not feel that her personal attention is required. Mrs. Wilson works in a factory.

---

[1] This chapter has been written by Mrs. Betty Davison.

It's a button factory, drilling sometimes and wrap parcels. I knew someone working there and she told me a vacancy and I went and asked. They pay me £4. 17s. 0d. less tax—I don't get a rebate and I understand I shouldn't be paying so much tax with so many children. Have written about it. I went to many places before I got this. I saw it in a paper, when I got there they say the vacancy gone and next day I saw it in the paper. There are no coloured there, pure white. That is why they wouldn't take me, pure white.

Mr. Wilson earns £12 a week and their weekly expenditure reads like this:

| | | | | | |
|---|---|---|---|---|---|
| £3. | 15s. 0d. | rent | £12. 0s. 0d. | Mr. Wilson |
| | 11s. 6d. | gas and oil | £4. 0s. 0d. | Mrs. Wilson |
| £4. | 0s. 0d. | to Jamaica | | |
| £3. | 0s. 0d. | food | | |
| £1. | 7s. 6d. | transport | | |
| £1. | 0s. 0d. | clothing | | |
| £2. | 6s. 0d. | baby things, etc. | | |
| £16. | 0s. 0d. | | £16. 0s. 0d. | |

This rent is dearer than the other one was, but the wall was sweating and the paper coming off. Catching cold every second. We're hoping to get a house at Hatfield, not come through as yet. It's a new settlement you know. Everybody put in before and so I will have to look about it. Have to wait two years, plenty of time now. At first nine months, then eighteen now five years here now. It will be much cheaper, three bedrooms and a sitting-room and it won't cost us £3. 15s. 0d. a week.

The thought of a larger house inevitably led to thoughts of the children and plans to bring them to England.

I want to try and send for two, the biggest children. I want them to get schooling, a proper place for them. I just like to fight me own self, not prey on anybody. I would like to get the big one to come, that way she could help herself, and the next one to go to school, just the money problem. Some really have money and don't want it, there's the foolishness, some dying for it and can't get it. All the children are beauties but you can't help them up. As far as we know, all right out there now, all we want is money to help them in school. They really don't pay fees, they go to Government school, just supply them with books, clothing and shoes. In school there now, when it comes to term set up and Granny goes ahead, have to send £5 or £6 when everybody make a change. Some two year in one class, so can't share books. Nothing charge, just cost me a lot. The only way to help the big one is to send her to dressmaking. She's making dresses for the smaller ones now, not so beautiful you know, but she can help them all.

A new, spotlessly clean cot and baby-bath crowded their well-kept room which, although my last visit was in June, was still decorated with their Christmas cards and photographs. The Wilsons were delighted with their new room, particularly as they explained:

We had to go to the public bath and now, just recently, just last week, they've fixed up a meter here. Sixpence or a shilling in the meter. We have a kitchen, share with another family up here, and a radio.

Mr. Wilson joined in the discussion here:

A friend, he have two [radios], one of the big ones with a spotlight, and he's going to give this one to his daughter and let us have it to lend. We have nothing at all in furniture. We stay at home, don't jump around much, we don't even have the money at the weekend to start anything. Just once a while we go to church, nothing, no show, nowhere. Can't afford to lose a shilling. Just go to church once awhile, not too much neither for only one suit. I never really take stock of what other people do, but with me personal, I don't like to wear one thing all the while. . . . I would like to go back to Jamaica, but not save a halfpenny, that's what's troubling me now. For honestly now, you see as far as I am concerned I real like Jamaica very much, but you know, you see the politicians run Jamaica into a wreck. Jamaica is more expensive than here now, such as clothing and even most food kinds too. You know, in Jamaica I don't eat bananas not four times in a week, you can't eat them all the while. The only thing I really miss Jamaica for is the mangoes. All those things are very nice, but the politics in Jamaica come to a standstill. A job is hard to pick up there now, overpopulated. If I could even say, could get somewhere convenient, I would go home to have the children under my protection. I would get a United Kingdom passport if I go to Jamaica, as I might want to come back. There are many who go back to Jamaica and then have to come back again. A man who was here six years and go back and start to do business. Good that he was good to his employer here, for he fixed up his papers for him to come back, he just spent his money foolishly. If we can bring the children to England, we will: not a surety, but we sadly miss them, but put up all the advantages. Granny will take best care of them. We live a life that anything we say to each other, we don't lie. If we tell her that we have no moneys to send to her, she don't feel anywhere hurt, she knows really there is none, for if we have it, she know she get it. You know our family not like plenty, we just understand what it is all about.

This struggling couple taped a message to their family in Jamaica for me to take back to them and it concluded:

Well, children, I long to see you, we have it very hard in England but by the mercy of God, one day, all of us will meet again. Give Granny my love and also good blessing for you in the name of Jesus. Good night.

## Mrs. Rocco

Mrs. Rocco is a staunch member of the Salvation Army, and I found her in London in a small room just large enough to hold a bed, dressing-table and wardrobe, everything as bright and gaily painted as possible in the dirty smoke-laden air which thickened the texture of the curtains, obliterating any colour or pattern. The view from the window was across a rubbish-packed yard to a row of identical houses about fifty yards away. Not a tree in sight, and only the grey vista of slate and brick to gaze upon.

A small, bright-eyed, dark-skinned woman, Mrs. Rocco had left her four children aged six, five, four and three in Jamaica with her husband. She was very distressed when I first visited her, for she had heard that two days after she had left Jamaica another woman with a month-old baby had moved into her home. She wrote and asked her husband about it, but he denied any improper association, claiming that he had employed the woman to look after the children. The neighbours and her sisters reported that this was not so, and caused havoc in Mrs. Rocco's life.

She had quickly established herself in England in the Salvation Army and at work. Walking past a dry-cleaning establishment one day she asked the doorman if they had any vacancies. He asked the manager, and she is still employed in the job he gave her as a 'spotter'. She is delighted that now she does not have to ask which chemical will remove which spot, and that the foreman said she was 'smart' to have learnt so quickly. The girls at work were knitting one day and offered to teach her.

Mrs. Rocco soon learnt, and showed me a case full of woollen cardigans that she had knitted and nylon underclothes she was sending to Jamaica for the children.

Mrs. Rocco rises at 5.45 every morning to catch a van which picks up a number of people and drops them off to meet a bus. Working overtime most nights, to earn more money, means she doesn't get home until 6.30 or 7 and then her busy home life begins. A meal is prepared and eaten, and personal laundry completed before she sets off to night school, where for the first year she studied English, Algebra, General Knowledge and Arithmetic. School books were proudly shown to me, and I read a delightful short essay on why she had come to England, the gist of which was that she wanted to make herself a better woman to offer more to Jamaica when she returns. She also showed me a set of three leather-bound books on general knowledge still kept in their box which she was buying for £6 on a weekly basis. Other nights she went to church activities, and has bought herself a Salvation Army bonnet, but she refuses to wear it without the uniform because: 'They wear other clothes you know. I'm going to buy a uniform; they never wear it that way, the uniform without the bonnet.' Her wish to conform to the group in the English society in which she lives is shown in her pride in not wearing the hat alone, but it will be some time before she will be able to afford the £12 or so that the uniform costs, and she feels on her return to Jamaica that the bonnet alone will suffice.

Life became gayer and happier for Mrs. Rocco when she left her tiny room and went to live with her brother. This well-kept room was much larger, and divided down the centre with a curtain threaded on a piece of string, each side of which was a three-quarter-size bed. Whenever I visited her, however, there were always two or three men with the brother, who may have been casual visitors or may have been making the most of the bed space available. Not many West Indians will turn a compatriot away if he is in need of a bed, food or a home.

A large radiogram and twenty-three-inch television set were run off the light, and the wires from these trailed down like streamers under the carpet to the appropriate appliance. This house was newly painted in vivid tones of blue and yellow and created a patchwork of pattern with the older dirty Victorian houses surrounding it.

During her second year Mrs. Rocco began her course in shorthand and typing, and went out much more with her brother and his friends.

We go to show [cinema] but don't fool around dance. Yes, we go to bingo and sometimes parties of other West Indians. They have a workers' club where I work, take threepence a week, go on an outing, or fairs and all that. We've been to Clacton-on-Sea and August coming we're going to Great Yarmouth. We went to Southend too.

Mrs. Rocco's husband in Jamaica is a salesman for office equipment, and although the woman who had moved in to live with him left and he moved with his children once or twice it seemed a most unsatisfactory arrangement, culminating in her husband being 'chopped' (stabbed) in his car in Kingston. The children were sent to live with Mrs. Rocco's mother as the father was unable to finance them for some time, and they were sent to school when possible.

The long hours Mrs. Rocco spent on her job earned her £7 per week, but 'some weeks go up to £8 with overtime. Well, you see, I don't pay tax, only 8s. 8d. for insurance.' She paid £2. 5s. 0d. for her half of the rent and spent approximately £3 on food. Mrs. Rocco was very grateful to her family for looking after her children, whom she loves dearly.

Since last month my mother have the children wholly so, but the month before that, the money I had in the bank—you know?—I drew that and give to my brother and sister £10 for the children and £20 was to finish paying for the school bill. I told you, I'm not in need of anything, I was doing general buying for myself all the while, I pay 2s. 6d. a week now and see if I can save. I don't promise like that you know, it's what I was saving, but sometimes I'll send Mother £2. Last year I did more saving, my husband send me £5 again and give me to buy a little thing. I wasn't paying much rent because only 30s. It wasn't a compulsion really I had to send money to the children then, but now I have to really.

Mrs. Rocco yawned and sniffed—she had a truly British common cold. 'Is it ten o'clock?' She put the clock to 11 p.m. and explained, 'I put it around fast; sometimes I oversleep and when I wake up and see the right time, I know I've got some to spare. I see six o'clock and it is only five.' Learning a sense of time the hard way, I thought, as I bade her good night and took the message for her family which I hoped to deliver in Jamaica. 'I don't know what time I will return to Jamaica, but I hope that I will return one day. I send good wishes to you all, good health and good courage.'

## Lorraine

Lorraine is of medium height, mid-brown skin and aged about thirty-four. When I met her in the Passport Office in Kingston in Jamaica she was very friendly and co-operative and obviously had organized her trip to England efficiently. She was going to a cousin already there who had promised to get her a job, and this eventually happened. In Jamaica she would do any work that came to hand: a little cooking, dressmaking or helping in the local shop, but it was difficult to obtain regular employment and when she came to me for her passport she was out of work.

On visiting her in London, I found her quite easily at the address she had given me in Jamaica, living with her cousin. She had worked for the first six months washing dishes in a railway cafeteria for less than £5 a week and found life difficult, and then worked inking shoes in a shoe factory for three months earning nearly £7 until, finally, she found employment as a domestic help in a hospital, where she still is, sometimes earning £8 a week with overtime.

Lorraine has always seemed to get on very well with people, at home in the house shared by about eight families, at work and with casual acquaintances met on the bus or in the shops. One day when she was shopping in the local Woolworths in Stoke Newington High Street, the English girl serving her took the trouble to chat and asked Lorraine where she came from, telling her that she must not pass her without speaking if she should meet her in the street. This delighted Lorraine, gave her a feeling of 'belonging' and enabled her to relax enough to chat to a casual acquaintance.

Lorraine was very distressed when the cousin with whom she lived was pushed down on the bus by a passenger who said, 'Get out of my way, you nigger'; she said that the cousin 'should have pushed her down back'. On the morning of the last day I visited her at work in the hospital, one of the patients had deliberately spilt rubbish on the floor. When Lorraine remonstrated with her the patient said, 'If I don't do that you won't have any work to do.' The other patients in the ward supported Lorraine, but she said, 'Today if only I could take a bus to go home to Jamaica, I would go. It is because you haven't got much money, then to make yourself better you have to come, and because people here feel that they have a little whiter skin, that they can take a liberty with you. I can't go back, I reach here already, so you have to make up your mind.' To go back to Jamaica she wants to be independent, to run her own little business and to have 'nobody curse me, or have abusing words to tell me'. Most Jamaican children, however poor, are brought up to be polite and well-mannered and this is rarely understood by the average English person.

The cousin with whom Lorraine had at first lived had a regular boy friend visiting her, and so although 'she was loving and very good' Lorraine felt that she had to move. She found another room through the 'agent for Jewry people'. According to Lorraine many houses in the area are owned by Jews who appoint West Indians as landlords and agents for sub-letting their property. Her new landlord and his whole family who occupied the house except for one single man, accepted Lorraine as a member of the family, and it was an exceedingly happy atmosphere in which to live.

When Lorraine was ill in bed with influenza for a week, she explained, 'Don't ever go down to the kitchen, everybody helped, and I got full wages, the National made it up.' This was a different story from when I visited her the first year, when she 'Couldn't stand being sick at home. I cried and cried with chilblains. When I stood on them they got hot and sore and my feet swell. . . . In Jamaica my foot was size six and now seven, not so big only tall. My hair fall off, fall off, I wouldn't have my photograph taken.'

Although the family were moving to the 'next place' they were taking Lorraine with them. She was most fortunate to be paying only £2 a week for her room which was bright and gay, with knick-knacks on the dressing-table and photographs in frames, not stuck in the mirror or crumpled and curling on the mantelpiece. She shared a cooker with the girl upstairs and paid a shilling for the hot-water geyser for a bath. One day when I visited her, I found her armed with a mop and pail, and rubber gloves, happily swabbing the floor while she chatted, taking her turn with the household to keep the communally used rooms and hallways clean.

Even with this new-found happiness in her home, Lorraine feels her life is very hard: 'The women work hard in England,' she said, 'but I haven't got the feeling to go back and work for someone else. I don't want someone above me barking me. If I had the money to settle down, a hundred pounds would do. I would have to start and do something.' She was very worried about her mother, who had 'cold in her feet, it takes so long to answer me, and she have I alone'. Lorraine does not write to anyone in Jamaica until she has had an answer to her letter, and so her communication with her family is spasmodic. She felt that the cousin in Jamaica who helped her financially to come to England, and who was thinking of coming herself, had better not come. 'She is easy to catch cold, and I prefer I know that she is there and not here sick. I am a little harder than she. You go out to work in the morning, it is so dark, and come home in the night.' She often works three hours' overtime to make her salary up to £7. 12s. 0d. and she puts aside £1 for Jamaica each week, but saves it up for a few weeks as: 'I can't send £1, looks too cheap.'

Lorraine continues to work hard, with hopes of returning to Jamaica with capital to start a business but she is still paying back the fare she borrowed to get to England in the first place, so the hopes must surely be wild dreams.

## Olga

Olga had been living in Spanish Town in Jamaica, staying at home with her baby girl and family although previously she had worked in a shop. She had not really wanted to emigrate, but her father had sent her the money for her fare, from England where he was living with a new wife, and at last she decided to go, leaving the baby with her own mother to look after in Jamaica.

A year after her arrival in England she was still desperately unhappy, embittered and longing to return to Jamaica. Her father, who had financed the trip, was anxious for her to do well, go to night school and better herself, and at first was very proud of her. He did not realize that during his four years in England his young daughter had grown up and did not wish to report to him on returning from the cinema, or have to get permission to stay out late. She had a child of her own and felt independent. Olga worked as a 'finisher' of trousers in an old house converted into a small clothing factory employing about fourteen people. It was dark, miserable and cold, with one dirty toilet, and she earned £5 a week. Relationships with her fellow workmates were good, but she did not respect her boss.

The winter weather proved too hard for Olga to continue to attend night school where she had started a course in shorthand and typing, so she discontinued it, and her whole life seemed thoroughly disorganized. She was unaware of how she spent her money, except that she remembered that she had to pay £10 for a winter coat and bought a number of woollies at £3 or £4 each. This however all changed in the second year of our survey during the second year of Olga's stay in England. She left the home of her father, who cut her out of his life and did not even know her address, and left the clothing factory. Here she had met a charming young man, Paul, from Antigua, and one day she 'tell him me going to come to live with him'. He agreed, they lived as man and wife, and although she was out of work for seven months he paid the rent, and looked after her while she cooked and kept the room tidy for him.

Paul was responsible for his sister's little girl, the sister having died, and a little boy of his own by a girl in Antigua. I asked Olga if she were jealous of the mother of Paul's child but she replied 'No, because I have a daughter by the next fellow.' Then Olga showed me a photograph of her little girl who 'didn't reach two yet. Mother take good care of her. I should send for her she wouldn't let her come—she loves her.' Olga unquestioningly accepts her mother's authority in this matter, and although she would love to see her daughter, willingly accepts the situation as it is. She told me that Paul says, 'If I buy something, I must buy something good', to send to his children and hers, as gifts to the West Indies. He earns £12 per week and she £6, so that life seemed much easier for Olga in these changed circumstances.

The room was about twelve feet square. Red linoleum shining and clean on the floor. A large treadle sewing-machine behind the door, used by Paul who is a tailor and does work at home. Flowered curtains, permanently drawn, darkened the room and the usual oil heater was balanced on its three legs

in the corner by the sealed-up fireplace. There was a clean
formica-topped table bearing a teapot and a bowl of oranges,
apples and ripe bananas. Olga said, 'It's very expensive over
here, fourpence for one banana, can get a dozen green ones
for fivepence in Jamaica.' The main part of the room was taken
up by a double bed covered by a clean gay pink bedspread and
used as a general seat and table. One rarely finds upholstered
or comfortable easy chairs in a migrant's home, but the beds
are often luxurious and beautifully clean. In Jamaica a bed
is considered a most important thing to own and many poor
people without enough to eat will get into desperate debt for
£30 to buy a bed which will often fill the wooden shack of a
room. It is considered an insurance, a status symbol and the
greatest joy in old age.

Olga's cooker was shared by another family on the same
floor, and the last visit I made one Sunday morning was inter-
rupted with her rushing intermittently to the stove to make sure
that her 'rice and peas' and curried chicken were not burning
. . . the Jamaican 'Sunday dinner' equivalent to the roast beef
and Yorkshire pudding of English families.

Questioned about her future, Olga was emphatic about her
desire to return to Jamaica and get a Jamaican passport.

Anytime I go back home, I am not coming back over here. If I
didn't know I wouldn't come. It isn't that I couldn't get a job.
Although you told me about the winds and the fog. A woman told me
that she left from here on Tuesday and never reach home till
Wednesday in the fog.

Then she thought of why she had left Jamaica and explained
that:

The father [of her little girl], he wanted to keep two [women] and
I didn't love that, so I drop meself off. If I win the pools I will go,
can't go home like I came. I want to know places, we stopped at
Canada on the way here and we liked it.

In the meantime Paul and Olga live happily on £18 a week
(less tax) in their one room, spending about £5 on food, £4 on
rent, light, baths and so on, and 10s. a week on rent for a
television, and regularly send money home to their families.
They do not seem to have any contact with English people, but
spend a great deal of time at home watching television and
visiting their West Indian friends.

Throughout the last interview there was a thumping loud music drumming from the room above so that we could hardly hear each other speak. When I mentioned it, Olga was the social critic.

He is coloured man from British Guiana, and she is a white girl— English. They play for the whole house, play 'til three in the morning, that same hour! You wouldn't do that in Jamaica except when you keep dance. Paul, he is a quiet boy, he wouldn't trouble them, we don't mess around with them, they got two dogs in their room

—and so Olga and Paul turn their television up louder to drown the noise from upstairs. The house was old, solidly built and in quite good repair, and this probably accounts for the fact that the noise did not penetrate into the tree-lined road.

## Ralph

Not all the visits we made to the immigrants resulted in reports of high endeavour. One night I knocked on the paint-peeled door of a very dirty-looking house, although it was in a broad tree-lined road in south-east London.

I knocked repeatedly, and waited; I was just about to push open the door and further my investigation when an extremely well-dressed young man confronted me. Enquiries about Ralph, the immigrant that I was visiting, were abortive as he had lived at this address for a very short time and left. I was then invited upstairs to the Jamaican's room, as he said that his friend there knew Ralph and he did not.

I followed the young man through the dirty, drab hallway and up the dark linoleum-covered stairs to the second floor and into a large room. Here I sank into the warm soft pile of carpet and was greeted by a very elegant young man who eased himself from the depths of a most luxurious off-white settee, where he had been reclining watching the largest television screen I have ever seen. Brocade curtains, a radiogram, and softly lit lamps gave the white and gold scene a 'film-set' atmosphere, but I was invited to enjoy one of the off-white chairs and when my mission was explained and the two young men heard that I had come from Jamaica they chatted amicably. They explained that they wanted English girl friends, and that they did not know the first thing about Ralph.

Realizing that they were using me to get introductions to English girls, I excused myself from their pressing invitations to stay, and they suggested that I should try some of the rooms downstairs to see if anyone knew of Ralph's present address.

I reached the ground floor and knocked on a door. A man's voice invited me to enter and I do not know who was the more surprised when I did. A man who looked like a light-skinned West Indian, aged about thirty-five to forty, lay on the bed in a satin dressing-gown, hair sleeked down, obviously expecting someone; he was very surprised at my appearance. I hastily withdrew, realizing that he would know nothing about Ralph; I understood that Ralph had left this house of iniquity that I had stumbled into as soon as he could after his arrival, and that Ralph was lost to the survey.

*Postscript*

8th February, 1965.
London, W.10.

Dear Mrs. Davison,

I do hope you are well. I do hope you remember me. I was living at . . . W.10. I am Elsie Jones (Mrs.). You send and interview me a few times.

Mrs. Davison I am asking you kindly to help me. Remember I told you I have a Son. I would like him to come to me in England. Mrs. Davison he is twenty years old. His name is Winston Jones.

Could you by any chance get a working voucher for him and also could you advise me. I was told to write to the High Commissioner in Jamaica. I wrote to him but I am not shore if everything is allright he has his Pass-Port just waiting. Please help me Mrs. Davison. Winston my Son has his Pass-Port I should also mension he lives at . . . Kingston 13, Jamaica W.I. Please write me back (Madam) and even give me some advise the money is ready to book his fare. I am just waiting and praying. Mrs. Davison he is my only Son my only child. Please help me, thanking you.

I am,
Yours Truly,
Elsie Jones

P.S. My madian [*sic*] name was Elsie Goodley.

# Appendix A

## LIST OF INTERVIEWERS

| | |
|---|---|
| Miss R. Ahmed | Birmingham |
| Mr. T. G. Ayre | Birmingham |
| Mr. E. T. Banks | London |
| Miss E. Beswick | Birmingham |
| Mr. F. Birch | London |
| Miss M. W. Blake | Northampton |
| Mr. A. Burchardt | London |
| Mrs. S. Burden | London |
| Miss A. B. Burton | Reading |
| Mrs. J. Carew | London |
| Miss D. Case | London |
| Mrs. M. Charnock | Birmingham |
| Mr. G. V. Compton | Derby |
| Mr. H. Cooper | Stoke-on-Trent |
| Mrs. C. S. Corteen | London |
| Miss B. Cowell | Doncaster |
| Mr. O. Daly | London |
| Mrs. B. Davison | London and Jamaica |
| Rev. C. E. Dawes | London |
| Mr. B. Dickens | Nottingham |
| Mr. M. Hinton | Oxford |
| Mr. A. Hutchinson | Newark |
| Mrs. V. Jackson | London |
| Mr. F. James | Nottingham |
| Mr. F. Laird | Nottingham |
| Mrs. L. E. Locke | London |
| Miss D. Lovesey | Walsall |
| Mr. T. R. Lunn | Leeds |
| Miss M. McDowell | Bedford |
| Mrs. M. Middlebrook Haigh | Huddersfield |
| Mrs. M. Muirie | Sheffield |
| Miss K. Norris | London |
| Mrs. M. O'Leary | Maidstone |
| Mrs. E. Rackham | London |
| Rev. J. Rimmer | Birmingham |
| Mr. C. E. B. Robinson | Leicester |
| Mr. S. E. Scott | Bradford |
| Mr. J. Shaw | London |
| Mrs. J. Shaw | London |
| Rev. H. Skinner | London |
| Mr. T. Stockton | Wolverhampton |

| | |
|---|---|
| Mrs. P. Thirlwell | London |
| Miss N. Uberoi | London |
| Miss E. Waldron | London |
| Father Walsh | Manchester |
| Miss S. Watson | London |
| Mr. S. J. Welsman | Bristol |
| Mrs. V. Williams | Watford |
| Miss D. M. Wood | Nottingham |

## *Appendix B*

### FINAL QUESTIONNAIRE

#### INSTITUTE OF RACE RELATIONS
36, Jermyn St., London, S.W.1

*Study of Jamaican Migration to Britain*
*Questionnaire No. 3*

NAME ........................................................

PASSPORT No.................................................

ADDRESS ....................................................

..........................................................

DATE OF COMPLETING QUESTIONNAIRE ............................

VISITOR ....................................................

---

(1) DATE OF ARRIVAL
On what date did informant arrive in England?

..........................................................

(2) CONTACT WITH JAMAICA

How frequently does informant communicate with family (or friends) in Jamaica?

|         | *Weekly or more often* | *Not weekly but at least once a month* | *Less than monthly* | *Never* |
|---------|---------|---------|---------|---------|
| Family  |         |         |         |         |
| Friends |         |         |         |         |

REMARKS: ...................................................
..........................................................

(3) STRUCTURE OF HOUSEHOLD

Is the informant LEGALLY married?

YES — Is he/she living with spouse at present? — YES  NO

NO — Is he/she living with another person as husband/wife? — YES  NO

REMARKS: ................................................
................................................
................................................

(4) RENT                    £   s.   d.
    (a)    What weekly rent does informant pay?
    (b)    What rooms and/or facilities does this cover?
           ................................................
           ................................................

REMARKS: ................................................
................................................

(5) LENGTH OF OCCUPATION
How long has the accommodation been occupied?

| Under one month | One month less than 3 months | 3 months less than one year | One year less than 3 years | 3 years or more |
|---|---|---|---|---|
| | | | | |

(6) HOUSEHOLD POSSESSIONS
Does the household possess, hire purchase, or rent any of the following?

| | Possess | Hire Purchase | Rent |
|---|---|---|---|
| Radio | | | |
| Television | | | |
| Motor car | | | |
| Motor cycle or Scooter | | | |
| Garage | | | |
| Refrigerator | | | |
| Electric iron | | | |
| Washing machine | | | |
| Cocktail cabinet | | | |
| Record player | | | |

REMARKS: ................................................
...............................................
...............................................

(7) LANDLORD

Nationality of Landlord

| Jamaican | English | Other (Specify) |
|---|---|---|

Jamaican

Is he a blood relative?

YES          NO

(8) SECURING EMPLOYMENT
How did informant find present (or last) employment?

| | |
|---|---|
| Through public employment exchange | |
| Through private agency paying a fee | |
| Through a friend (no fee) | |
| Response to advertisement | |
| Personal application on chance | |

If none of the above, state the method used:
..................................................
..................................................

(9) HOURS WORKED
How many hours were worked in the last complete week (Sunday to Saturday) of work?

| Normal Hours | Overtime | Supplementary Employment | Travelling Time |
|---|---|---|---|
| | | | |

REMARKS: ................................................
...............................................
...............................................
...............................................

(10)  TRADE UNION
Is informant a member of a British trade union?

```
                          |
         ┌────────────────┴────────────────┐
         |                                 |
        YES                               NO
         |                                 |
   Which union?                  Ever been asked to join?
   ....................              ┌──────┴──────┐
         |                           |             |
Ever attended a branch meeting?     YES           NO
   ....................
         |
   Holds any office?
```

YES.................................
(specify)
   ..................................
NO ................................
REMARKS:  .........................................................
.................................................................
.................................................................


(11)  INCOME TAX RELIEFS
Has informant applied for income tax reliefs for children left in
Jamaica?

```
                          |
         ┌────────────────┴────────────────┐
         |                                 |
        YES                               NO
         └──────────Have they been obtained?
                          |
         ┌────────────────┴────────────────┐
         |                                 |
        YES                               NO
                                  Why have they been refused?
                                  ─────────────────────────
                                           |
                                  No birth certificate? ........
                                  No marriage certificate? ....
                                  No letter from J.P. in
   REMARKS:  ...............      Jamaica? ..................
   ..........................     Other reasons  ...........
   ..........................     ..........................
   ..........................     ..........................
   ..........................     ..........................
   ..........................     ..........................
```

(12)  PARTNER AND CREDIT UNION
Does the informant belong to any form of co-operative savings group,
e.g. the Partner, or Credit Union?

|                  | IN JAMAICA | IN BRITAIN |
|------------------|------------|------------|
| Partner          |            |            |
| Credit Union     |            |            |

REMARKS: .................................................
..........................................................
..........................................................

(13)  RETURN TO JAMAICA

PLANS TO RETURN

YES                                    NO

Within 5          Sometime
years             indefinite

Any money saved towards return fare?

YES               NO

REMARKS: .................................................
..........................................................
..........................................................

(14)  ATTITUDE TO JAMAICA
Does the informant think that he/she could settle down to life in
Jamaica again?

..........................................................
..........................................................
..........................................................

(15)  PASSPORT
On renewal of his/her passport does informant intend to obtain a
Jamaican or a U.K. passport?

Jamaican                              U.K.

REMARKS: ..............................................
......................................................
......................................................

(NOTE: After five years' residence in this country a Jamaican can register as a U.K. citizen and obtain a U.K. passport.)

(16) CHILDREN IN JAMAICA
How many children (15 years of age and under) for which the informant is responsible have been

                                 *Number*
       (a) brought to England?     ........
       (b) left in Jamaica?       ........

REMARKS: ..............................................
......................................................
......................................................

(17) CHILDREN
If children have been left behind in Jamaica is it intended to bring them to England?

YES             NO        DO NOT KNOW

REMARKS: ..............................................
......................................................
......................................................

(18) CHILDREN IN JAMAICA
Is any anxiety felt about the welfare of children left in Jamaica?

YES             NO        NOT APPLICABLE

REMARKS: ..............................................
......................................................
......................................................

(19) Please give address of Guardian of children in Jamaica.
*Names of Children*...........................................
......................................................
......................................................
*Name of Guardian*...........................................
*Address of Guardian in Jamaica*...............................
......................................................
REMARKS: ..............................................
......................................................

(20) CHILDREN IN ENGLAND
Has the informant one or more child/children under 5 years of age living with him/her in England?

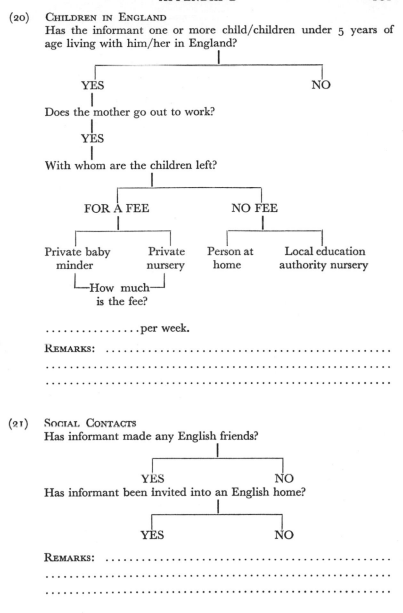

YES           NO

Does the mother go out to work?

YES

With whom are the children left?

FOR A FEE       NO FEE

Private baby minder    Private nursery    Person at home    Local education authority nursery

—How much— is the fee?

. . . . . . . . . . . . . . . per week.

REMARKS: . . . . . . . . . . . . . . . . . . . . . . . . . . . . . . . . . . . . . . . . . . . . . . . .
. . . . . . . . . . . . . . . . . . . . . . . . . . . . . . . . . . . . . . . . . . . . . . . . . . . . . . . . . . . .
. . . . . . . . . . . . . . . . . . . . . . . . . . . . . . . . . . . . . . . . . . . . . . . . . . . . . . . . . . . .


(21) SOCIAL CONTACTS
Has informant made any English friends?

YES           NO
Has informant been invited into an English home?

YES           NO

REMARKS: . . . . . . . . . . . . . . . . . . . . . . . . . . . . . . . . . . . . . . . . . . . . . . . .
. . . . . . . . . . . . . . . . . . . . . . . . . . . . . . . . . . . . . . . . . . . . . . . . . . . . . . . . . . . .
. . . . . . . . . . . . . . . . . . . . . . . . . . . . . . . . . . . . . . . . . . . . . . . . . . . . . . . . . . . .


(22) LEISURE
Does the informant habitually attend any of the following recreational activities?

*(Please tick in the appropriate square)*

| | |
|---|---|
| (a)  Public House | |
| (b)  Cinema | |
| (c)  Public Dance Hall | |
| (d)  Football or similar sport | |
| (e)  Dog or horse racing | |
| (f)  Bingo sessions | |
| (g)  West Indian parties | |
| (h)  Evening classes | |

(23)  CHURCH
Is the informant a member of any religious group?

YES          NO

Where do the meetings
take place?

In a church building     In a private house

What is it called?

..................................

REMARKS:  ...............................................
...........................................................
...........................................................

(24)  HOLIDAY
What did informant do during his/her annual holiday from work last year?

...........................................................
...........................................................
...........................................................

(25)  SOURCES OF HELP AND ADVICE
Has the informant ever made use of the services of any social service agency (e.g. Citizens' Advice Bureau, Welfare Department of Local Authority, W.V.S., Red Cross, Jamaica Migrant Service Office, etc.)?

```
         ┌────────────────────────┴──────────────┐
       YES                                       NO
        │                           ┌─────────────┴─────────────┐
Specify which agencies             │                           │
. . . . . . . . . . . . . . . . .        Not needed              Not known
. . . . . . . . . . . . . . . .
REMARKS:  . . . . . . . . . . . . . . . . . . . . . . . . . . . . . . . . . . . . . . . . . . . .
. . . . . . . . . . . . . . . . . . . . . . . . . . . . . . . . . . . . . . . . . . . . . . . . . .
. . . . . . . . . . . . . . . . . . . . . . . . . . . . . . . . . . . . . . . . . . . . . . . . . .
```

## DEGREE OF SETTLEMENT

At the conclusion of the interview you are asked to attempt to assess the degree of settlement (i.e. the extent to which problems have been solved in several spheres of social life).

The following code should be used:

"A"—The individual has no observable problems.

"B"—There are problems but there is reasonable hope of solution within the near future.

"C"—The problems are considerable and there is no immediate sign of solution.

"D"—Hopeless.

Please consider the individual interviewed in relation to each of the following aspects of his life and tick "A", "B", "C", or "D" according to your assessment of the situation.

|  | A | B | C | D |
|---|---|---|---|---|
| Domestic Life |  |  |  |  |
| Housing |  |  |  |  |
| Employment |  |  |  |  |
| Church |  |  |  |  |
| English Community |  |  |  |  |
| Jamaican Community |  |  |  |  |

DATE. . . . . . . . . . . . . . . . . . . . . .    SIGNED. . . . . . . . . . . . . . . . . . . .
*Visitor*

# INDEX